Christmastime in KANSAS CITY

THE STORY OF THE SEASON

Monroe Dodd

KANSAS CITY STAR BOOKS

Kansas City, Missouri

Design:
Jean Dodd

Published by KANSAS CITY STAR BOOKS
1729 Grand Blvd.
Kansas City, Missouri, USA 64108

All rights reserved
Copyright 2001 the Kansas City Star Co.

No part of this book may be reproduced, stored in a retrieval system or transmitted in any form or by any means electronic, mechanical, photocopying, recording or otherwise, without the prior consent of the publisher.

First edition
Library of Congress Card Number: 2001119601
ISBN: 0-9712920-7-8

Printed in the United States of America
by Walsworth Publishing Co., Marceline, Mo.

Requests for permission to make copies of any part of the work should be mailed to StarInfo, c/o The Kansas City Star, 1729 Grand Blvd., Kansas City, MO 64108. To order additional copies, call StarInfo (816) 234-4636 and say "Operator." Or visit our Web site at www.kcstarinfo.com.

Dust jacket photograph: Front: Petticoat Lane at night, early 1960s, looking west. Back: Decorated home in December 1990, 86th Terrace and Lamar Avenue, Overland Park.

Endsheets: An assortment of toys and Christmas memorabilia from the Toy & Miniature Musuem of Kansas City and the Kansas City Museum/Union Station.

Introductory photographs:
i: Children watched the Santa Claus parade parade downtown on Nov. 30, 1929.
ii-iii: 1000 block of Main Street at night, looking north, early 1960s.
v: Petticoat Lane looking east, December 1959.
vi-vii: Country Club Plaza Christmas lights, early 1990s.
viii: At the lighting ceremony for the Salvation Army Tree of Lights, 3637 Broadway, in November 1999.
x: A cowboy outfit for Christmas, mid-1950s.
xi: An encounter with Santa in late November 1999 at Metro North Shopping Center.
xii: Decorated home in December 1990, 86th Terrace and Lamar Avenue, Overland Park.
xiv-1: Hallmark wrapping paper from the 1950s.

TABLE OF CONTENTS

Introduction 2
1. On the frontier 4
2. Stirring up business: 1850-1865 14
3. Hustle and bustle: 1866-1890 28
4. A season for charity: 1890-1918 42
5. Dressed in holiday style: 1919-1945 64
6. All our Christmases: 1946-2000s 98
   "The Best Christmas Story of Them All" by Bill Vaughan 156

Afterword 159

Acknowledgments, bibliography 160
Illustration sources 161
Index 162

The Santa Claus float on Grand Avenue in the downtown Christmas parade, 1929.

"It has been an instinct in nearly all peoples, savage or civilized, to set aside certain days for special ceremonial observances, attended by outward rejoicing. This … answers to man's need to lift himself above the commonplace and the everyday, to escape from the leaden weight of monotony …. Festivals are as sunlit peaks, testifying, above dark valleys, to the eternal radiance."

— *Clement A. Miles,* Christmas in Ritual and Tradition, Christian and Pagan, *published in London in 1912.*

Introduction

Christmastime is an annual festival of frenzy. These days, it can span six weeks. It starts innocently, and then social life gathers steam, families gather to bond, and business colleagues slap backs and exchange cards and trinkets and well wishes.

The season delivers happy music, bright light, good feelings and kindness just as the year is turning cold and grim. Food is rich and tasty, and there's plenty of it. The yearly exchange of gifts among relatives and friends means most folks will finish the holiday with more personal possessions than they had when it began.

At the same time, Christmas delivers something else: A drumbeat of advertising that annually blurs the finer elements and seems sometimes to corrupt the lofty motives of the season, a hollow sense that the season can never be as good as memory and hope predict, guilt over missed opportunities, hangovers, bills.

Christmas is a whirl of contradictory visions. It's a clash of optimism and cynicism that afflicts most adults each year. Yet the affliction never stops us from marching right ahead and having another Christmas and then another.

Perhaps the real magic of Christmas is its staying power. Over the centuries, Christmas was transformed from a pagan year-end festival into a religious commemoration. Yet it never fully lost its status as a boisterous public free-for-all. To combat excess, 19th-century society reconceived Christmas as a family occasion. The full bloom of the industrial age loaded the season with commercial meaning and laid the groundwork for renewed public celebration.

Despite its many changes of shape and purpose, its warring values of faith and fun and profit, the holiday has survived and prospered. Rowdy or religious, the season has represented a way for human beings to alter their ordinary behavior — and in an almost magical way. As author Stephen Nissenbaum points out in *The Battle for Christmas*, the occasion reveals "something of what we would like to be, what we once were, or what we are becoming despite ourselves."

Clearly, the Christmas season continues to exist as the most anticipated time of the year. Clearly, that springs from our overall success in satisfying desires and emotional needs, as James H. Barnett wrote almost half a century ago in his book, *The American Christmas*. The definition of this holiday embodies some basic, universally admired values — chief among them brotherhood and family life and human kindness.

In Kansas City, in the heart of the Great Plains, the Christmas season shows all these characteristics. Through hard times and good, through war and peace, through frontier hardship and modern affluence, the metropolis has nourished a Christmas season that matches any city's.

This is the story of how the Christmas season has been marked in these parts.

Naturally, no one can hope to tell all the ways we have celebrated Christmas over the years. After all, there are as many Kansas City Christmases as there are charities and churches and families and people — and there are more than 1½ million of us at last count. But we can recall the big stories and touch on the small ones.

That brings us to our starting point. In this part of the world, Christmas celebrations began one and three-quarter centuries ago. And they, like the settlement that became Kansas City, emerged quite small…

1

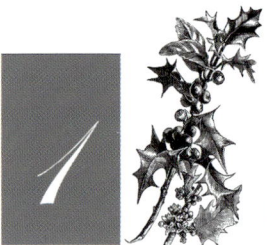

On the frontier

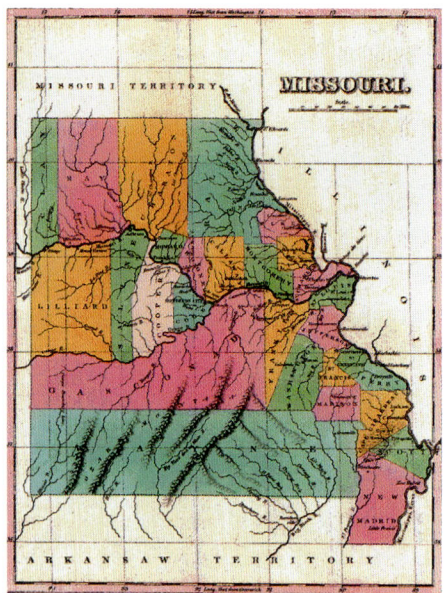

Missouri in the early 1820s.

In 1821, the same year Missouri entered the Union, a small band of French-speaking fur traders and trappers settled along the Missouri River near the western border of the new state. They erected wood buildings downstream from Kawsmouth, where the Kansas, or Kaw, flowed into the Missouri.

Here, at the mouth of the Kansas River, an imaginary north-south line formed the western boundary of the United States. This frontier region was heavily forested in the lowlands and prairie on the highlands, inhabited by members of the Osage nation, a sprinkling of the French-speakers and in years to come an English-speaking pioneer family or two. Immediately to the west lay the vast unsurveyed lands of the rest of the Louisiana Purchase.

For all who lived here, life amounted to a continual confrontation with heat and cold, with flood and drought, with rock, dust, mud and forest undergrowth.

If Christmas was much celebrated, the earliest settlers left precious little evidence of it.

Not many generations removed from France, the heritage of the Roman Catholics who settled near Kawsmouth would have called for a creche to be built in the living area of homes. The children's shoes would have been left before the fireplace to be filled by the Christ Child, *le petit Jesu*. The settlers would have gathered for midnight Mass, followed by an early-morning meal.

But this was not France, nor even St. Louis, settled for more than six decades by the relatives of many of these French-speakers. Until the early 1830s, there could be no midnight Mass at Kawsmouth, because there was no priest.

Small festivity, stern disapproval

Chief among the earliest settlers were Francois and Berenice Chouteau, children of upper-class families of eastern Missouri and western Illinois. The Chouteaus could have brought to this wilderness some vestige of the Christmas

A time for making merry

For centuries in northern latitudes, the last few weeks of the year were a season for celebration. As the year wound down, the sun traveled its lowest arc through the sky. After solstice it began to rise. Daylight reached its briefest period, then began to grow longer. Year's end meant the harvest was done, and the onset of cold meant farm tasks were over. Winter weather also meant meat animals could be easily preserved after slaughter. Supplies of beer and wine were ready. Feasting was in order.

The Romans marked the period with Saturnalia, hailed as a time of abundance and rebirth. To the north, Scandinavians called their season of renewal Yule. These were times for banquets, strong drink, gambling, licentiousness — often done to excess. They were times for riotous living.

Sometime in the middle of the fourth century, the leaders of the Western branch of Christianity decided to set a date to mark the birth of Jesus Christ. Historians say the church may have hoped to draw Roman revelers and sun-worshippers to Jesus, or may have been trying to add to Jesus a human quality by establishing for him a human date of birth. Evidently, the Christians believed they could co-opt this time of celebration.

The writers of the Gospels in the Christian Bible had given little hint as to the day Jesus was born. They indicated that the birth occurred when shepherds were in the field, watching their flocks — springtime.

Despite that clue, the church chose a date far from spring, one in the few days between the festivals of Saturnalia and the Roman New Year's holiday, Kalends. They chose the winter solstice according to the Julian calendar — Dec. 25. They named it the Feast of the Nativity.

Already, Christians were celebrating Epiphany, commemorating the revelation of Jesus' divinity to those around him, on Jan. 6. Now that a date was chosen to celebrate Christ's birth, Epiphany stayed on the church calendar; the Western branch of Christianity marked it as the revelation of Jesus' divinity to the Magi, the three kings who came to visit the baby. To the Eastern church, Epiphany was dedicated to Jesus' baptism. Twelve days lay between the two dates, spawning the Twelve Days of Christmas and Twelfth Night.

The church had placed a heavenly layer over the wild and worldly celebrations of year's end. Yet those revelries, the church found, could not be eliminated. And despite the best efforts of many churchmen, the fusion of sacred and profane at Christmastime lingered for centuries — and never really was eliminated.

ON THE FRONTIER

Fort Osage

Before statehood

A government-authorized post for trading with the Osage was established in northeast Jackson County in 1808. It was called Fort Osage, and its factor, or agent, was George Sibley. He noted the passage of Christmas in his diary, but little else. In 1810, Dec. 25 had fair weather with only a bit of snow remaining on the ground. "A very pleasant day," Sibley wrote. "This is the third Christmas that I have passed at Fort Osage." How he passed the day otherwise, Sibley did not say.

practice, perhaps in their home. Yet in letters written to Berenice Chouteau's family over the years, Francois Chouteau made only scant mention of Christmas and none of celebration.

In early November 1829, Chouteau wrote that Indians with whom he traded would return from their hunt for furs "around Christmas." A few years later he reported that the trader William Gillis had stirred the wrath of the local Indian agent by delivering 7 gallons of whiskey to Indians on Christmas Day and by having an associate "frolic with them." When a child was born to the Chouteaus on Christmas Day 1828, the coincidence of the date was not remarked upon.

Not until 1833, six years after Jackson County was organized and Independence was made its seat, did a priest arrive. That year, Father Benedict Roux held the first service for the Catholic settlement at Kawsmouth — on Christmas day.

An English-speaking settler — Roux referred to him only as "an American Protestant" — lent the priest his house for the Christmas-Day services. Roux gave a sermon — first in French and then in English, but he

Christmas: Against it or for it?

In the 1600s, the Puritans of England tried to stamp out Christmas celebrations altogether. They pointed to the artificiality of the date, Dec. 25, considering the setting of it presumptuous. They recoiled at paganlike excesses that marked the season — drinking and gluttony, gambling, dancing, and noisemaking. A tradition dating back to Rome held that year's end could be marked by reversing social standings. The Puritans believed that custom, however temporary, led to a mocking of authority.

Puritan leaders set stern rules.

This opposition crossed the Atlantic, and the Puritans of New England likewise tried to purify their part of the New World, to bring order to a time of misrule. Through the 1600s and 1700s American Puritans were joined by Congregationalists, Baptists, Presbyterians and Quakers in strongly opposing even a religious observance of Christmas. They had an additional reason: the Church of England did mark Christmas. Because of that, the holiday became lumped in the same political bag with British royal officials and Toryism in politics. As colonial anger grew at the dominance of the mother country in American matters, opposing Christmas came to be linked with opposition to the despised king.

However, this dim view of year-end festivity was not shared by American colonists to the south. In Virginia, Maryland and the Carolinas, church leaders and officialdom accepted a leisurely period of festivities and play — cards, ninepins, horse racing, and home entertaining — from Christmas to New Year's. Derided in New England, noisemaking was an important element of the holiday in the Middle Atlantic and the South. Usually it was accomplished by firing guns. Another widespread custom was drinking and drunkenness.

By the end of the 1700s, the Puritan ban on observance was beginning to fade in the Northeast. There, ministers of various faiths began to support a religious observance of Christmas, hoping that the excesses of the secular holiday could be kept under control. But as the 19th century dawned, such dreams were losing ground in New England. Across America, Christmas was now an acknowledged part of year-end revelry. The celebration could not be stifled.

ON THE FRONTIER

A Jesuit priest and inveterate artist, Father Nicolas Point sketched the log church where he served from late 1840 to spring 1841. It was called St. Francis Regis and stood atop the bluffs near Kawsmouth. Wagons in the foreground were heading south to Westport.

"There were no lack of ills awaiting cure. What with the ignorance of some, the drunkenness of others, the sensuality of almost all, there was misery enough."

— *Father Nicolas Point*

did not celebrate Mass, because he feared "Americans" might somehow act irreverent. Then events took a sour turn, at least by the priest's lights. That very evening the man who donated the building for the service staged a *bal* — a dance!

"He is a great lover of balls," Roux wrote, "and took advantage of our Christmas meeting to give one. I do not care to furnish him an occasion of doing a thing against which I have openly declared and will continue ever so to do." For Father Roux, neither Christmas nor any other day should be defiled by dancing.

Yet balls had been a regular feature of life at Kawsmouth before the priest arrived, and his parishioners took issue with him. Among the objectors were the Catholic community's staunchest financial backers, the Chouteaus. By 1835 the priest was gone.

Whether Roux was too strict or the settlers too rowdy was unclear, but a clue to the state of things came from the memoirs of the next priest to arrive, Nicolas Point.

"There were no lack of ills awaiting cure," Point recalled of his time at Kawsmouth in 1840 and 1841. "What with the ignorance of

Santa Claus

St. Nicholas' popular linkage with Christmas began early in the 19th century with a boost from Washington Irving. His *History of New York* — which really was a quasi-history that partly invented a world to fit the city's original Dutch settlers — designated Nicholas as the patron saint of New York. St. Nicholas had been popular in the Netherlands.

In 1823, the Santa Claus legend got its biggest boost when the *Troy Sentinel* in New York published "An Account of a Visit from St. Nicholas." By the late 1820s the poem was being printed widely in U.S. newspapers, and it was published in book form in 1844. Illustrations of a Santa that looked like the one in "A Visit from St. Nicholas" were appearing by the late 1830s.

The myth of this St. Nicholas not only was attractive — "a right jolly old elf" who magically traveled the world — but also the saint proved useful to parents. Good children were supposed to get presents, bad children switches or other unpleasant gifts.

Illustrations of a Santa that looked like the one described in "A Visit from St. Nicholas" were appearing by the late 1830s.

Santa as depicted in the first edition in book form of "A Visit from St. Nicholas." It was published in 1848 under the name of Clement C. Moore, although Moore's authorship later was questioned.

The best known Santa Claus illustrator, Thomas Nast, first illustrated an edition of "A Visit" in 1863. During the Civil War, he depicted Santa distributing gifts to Union soldiers in their camps. After the Civil War, Nast created a world for Santa to inhabit: A workshop, his telescope for spotting good children, his home, his ice palace.

ON THE FRONTIER

Scraping by

Holiday spending was a concern, even in the mid-1840s. Consider this item, published in 1846 in *The Tribune* of Liberty:

"At all times it is unpleasant and inconvenient to be poor, but especially so just about this season of the year, when the holidays require a fellow to appear in bandbox trim, and with pockets snugly lined with 'kilter.' O! how we would like to possess the 'wherewith,' i.e., the dimes. How we would spread smiles over the countenances of our friends, with good Christmas cheer, and make all the little ones in the burg roar with laughter at the funny freaks of old Santa Claus. Well, ours is the poor poet's wish, that 'a dime would grow like scandal — bigger and bigger the more it circulates.'"

Toys of the times: With luck, a frontier child might have gotten this tin kitchen and accessories for Christmas about 1850.

some, the drunkenness of others, the sensuality of almost all, there was misery enough."

In this part of the world, Point wrote, "man's licentious nature brooked no bounds."

It's not surprising that the frontier was a rough-and-tumble place. Settlers typically arrived with one thing in mind — making money. Kawsmouth provided two big opportunities for income.

Native American tribes — Shawnee, Delaware and others — were being paid by the government to leave their land in the East and resettle in the territory just west of Missouri. These tribes had money to spend with entrepreneurs who set up shop along the border, in new towns like Westport.

Other Americans were making money from the trade with Santa Fe in northern Mexico, at the other end of the long trail that in 1821 began in central Missouri. In the 1830s, traders started to use a Missouri River landing near Kawsmouth to equip and set off on their overland journey. The region became an emporium of the West.

By 1840, Father Point was characterizing it as "the gathering point for all expeditions to Mexico,

California and the Rocky Mountains."

Despite the priest's concern at the area's roughhewn character, he managed to equip the church so that at Christmas the community "was enabled to enjoy all those blessings of religion which we could have looked for only in a larger city." As for the balls, Father Point countenanced two dances in his five-month tenure, and those he put up with "lest by too great severity I might lose the ground I had gained" with the settlers.

Celebration

The balls and the spirit they represented would win the day. This announcement, with a standoffish editorial comment, appeared in *The Tribune* of Liberty in Clay County on Dec. 17, 1847:

"A ball will be given at the Eagle Hotel in this place on Christmas Eve. Although we do not participate in amusement of this kind, we hesitate not in saying to those who are fond of 'plying the fantastic toe' that things will be done up in style. Attend and see! The Dover Brass Band, we are informed, will be present."

Not only was dancing allowed, but also it was used for town-building.

In church

Questions about the propriety of Christmas worship lasted well into the 19th century. The Sunday School movement spread rapidly among Protestant denominations in the early 1800s, but printed materials devised for multiple denominations at first made little mention of Christmas. The publisher, the American Sunday School Union, feared backlash from some of the denominations it served. By 1859, however, the Sunday School literature contained accounts of Christmas celebrations, hymns and other references to the season. By 1870, Christmas had become an accepted lesson topic.

Through much of the 1800s Christian churches differed in the way they marked Christmas. Denominations that traditionally supported Christmas held morning services on the day. That group included Episcopalians and Lutherans. Roman Catholic churches celebrated a midnight mass and several masses on Christmas morning. Baptists, Presbyterians, Methodists and Congregationalists — all of which had once been hostile to Christmas celebrations of any kind — began to mark the day on the nearest Sunday.

In 1841, Liberty had held a series of December cotillions to raise money for a library.

Unlike the earliest settlers at Kawsmouth, most residents of Clay and Jackson counties were non-Catholics from states such as Kentucky, Virginia or Tennessee and thus not subject to the admonitions of a disapproving priest. As the fur trade declined in the 1830s, the number of English-speakers rapidly overwhelmed the French-speaking community.

For these new settlers, Christmas presumably would have been a reproduction of what they had known in their native states:

CHRISTMASTIME IN KANSAS CITY

ON THE FRONTIER

Youthful revelry

In 1827, the *Missouri Intelligencer* was the westernmost newspaper published in Missouri. Its office in Fayette lay 100 miles from Kawsmouth — a voyage of several days by river, longer over land. In an extended Christmastime reverie of that year, the editor touched on the ways of youth — and counseled elders to be tolerant:

"The blooming young men are distributing Ball Tickets to our wives and daughters. The latter … commence a host of preparations, in preparing their headdresses, twisting their curls, and starching and crimping their colaretts, and in arranging all the fancy trappings of female attire …."

"While our sons and daughters are vying with each other in the joyous and mazy dance, exhilarated by the sweet tones of the violin or the tinkling cymbal, let us not censure too harshly. We, too, were once young …. When they are old, they will cease to delight in its amusements."

A cup of cheer

Drink was for many years an essential part of Christmas — in some sectors the primary part. The editor of *The Tribune* in Liberty made no secret of his anticipation in this article, published in mid-December 1846:

"Christmas comes but once a year; therefore we must indulge in eggnogs and jollifications to our heart's content next week. We have already commenced puckering our mouths for the delicious beverage."

Southern-style occasions spent at home, with turkey or venison cooked over large fireplaces, accompanied by dried vegetables or fruits. Noisemaking was important in southern Christmases, so gunfire surely was a part of the celebration.

One ex-Southerner whose family traditions were passed down through the decades was James H. Compton, a Virginian who moved two log cabins together in 1844 to make a four-room house on a hill seven miles west of Liberty. Compton prospered; the home was expanded over the years and it stayed in the family until the late 1930s. In 1938 Emma Leta Compton recalled in a newspaper article that family custom called for corn cakes and maple syrup on Christmas morning. If streams were frozen, a chunk of ice was cut, the syrup heated and poured on the ice, which it penetrated. Once hardened by the cold, Compton said, the syrup was withdrawn and the result was "treacle," an old-fashioned version of an all-day sucker.

In the 1840s, wild turkey for the Christmas feast was still plentiful in the woods around the Compton home. Clay and Jackson counties were largely agrarian outposts of the frontier, and Liberty, Independence and Westport were small towns. Christmases were mostly domestic matters, untouched by public spectacle and almost entirely absent of commercial exploitation.

In the next decade, that was going to change. A new territory would emerge to the west and a new city would spring up at Kawsmouth. The quiet, simple and little-remarked frontier Christmas would vanish.

To be a child once more!

Alfred S. Waugh, an artist whose only surviving work apparently is his memoir of life in the West, *Travels in Search of the Elephant*, came to western Missouri hoping to join John C. Fremont's expedition to the West. Failing in that, he shared time between Independence and Lexington in Lafayette County, making portraits and busts of local people. These are his thoughts about Christmas Day 1845, which he spent in Independence, bitterly cold:

"Christmas — that season so dear to young hearts. Oh! how the approach of that festival used to look to me in my young days, so fraught with happiness....When I think of my early days...I am ready to burst out in the words of the song: 'Oh would I were a boy again.'

"But what's the use of sighing?"

2 | 1850-1865
Stirring up business

As was customary in the Clay County seat of Liberty, a Christmas ball would be held the night of the holiday in 1851. The managers of the Eagle Hotel, according to *The Tribune*, "intend to give everybody a sight for their money."

In the same item, the managers also indulged in some cross-promotion of their big dance.

"They would also recommend those wishing to purchase jewelry to the establishment of J. Purley. His is the only house in Liberty where you can find anything that is fine and cheap. He has just received another large and splendid assortment of ladies' breast pins, finger rings and earrings. Call quick as they are going off fast."

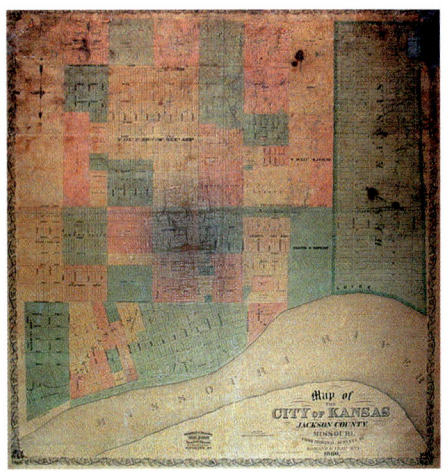

In this 1860 map of Kansas City, south was at the top.

Merchants were catching on to the commercial possibilities of the holiday. The Liberty Book Store, in an advertisement that was first published in *The Tribune* on Nov. 28, boasted that it had received a "splendid assortment" of annuals and gift books "suitable for Christmas and New Year's presents."

Surviving records of a store in Sibley in northeast Jackson County, Mo., show that on Dec. 13, 1854, Dennis Sanders bought a side saddle for $16, which is worth about $300 in 2001 money. It was the most costly item purchased in the month of December at that store, and it was probably a gift for Sanders' wife or daughter (in the same shopping trip, Sanders bought ribbon).

The merchants of western Missouri had much to look forward to in holiday seasons to come. With 1854 came removal of Indian tribes from their

14   CHRISTMASTIME IN KANSAS CITY

Dances marked the Christmas season across the frontier West.

1850-1865: STIRRING UP BUSINESS

Slavery

Missouri was a slave state, and until the Civil War most black Missourians were slaves. The state had few farms that reached the scale of Southern plantations — the majority of Jackson County slaveholders in 1860 had three or fewer slaves — yet most Missouri slaves worked as field hands. Others, were valets, butlers, handymen, laborers, maids, nurses and cooks.

For slaves, Christmas brought extended time off from work — sometimes as much as a month — and so the season was recalled fondly by many as a temporary escape from servitude. The time was marked by dancing, feasting and drinking.

One former slave, interviewed in the mid-1930s when he was 92 years old, recalled holiday time on a farm near Jefferson City. From Christmas time well into January, Gus Smith and his fellow slaves got "a whole month to go and come as much as we pleased and go for miles as we wanted to, but we had better be back by the first of February."

Smith recalled holiday meals of "all kinds of game, ducks, geese, squirrels, rabbits, possum, pigeons and fried chicken …. Great big pound cakes a foot and a half high."

"White folks and colored folks came to these gatherings, from miles around, sat up all night dancing and drinking," Smith said. "We always had our own musicians. Sometimes we'd send 10 or 12 miles for a fiddler. He'd stay a week or so in one place and then go on to the next farm."

Other slaveowners were less generous. Ex-slave George Jackson Simpson, born in Crawford County in southeast Missouri in 1854, recalled he was allowed only one week off.

"That was the only holiday we had," he said, "but we did well to get that in those days."

In other places, the celebration came under the auspices

The yule log being dragged to the hearth.

of the slave owner, who strictly controlled matters, even to doling out alcohol. Many owners apparently believed such celebrations gave slaves an outlet for dissatisfaction and bought peace. The abolitionist crusader Frederick Douglass agreed, saying such holidays "were among the most effective means in the hands of slaveholders of keeping down the spirit of insurrection among the slaves."

A common Christmastime practice in Missouri and in other slave states was the acquisition of a yule log, typically a large branch or tree trunk burned in an open-hearth fireplace. As the end of the log burned down, it was pushed farther in to the flames. Some slave owners are said to have allowed the slaves' holiday to continue as long as the log burned, so the slaves selected the largest and greenest log they could find. Often, the stories said, the log was soaked in a pond — an attempt to make the log burn as slowly as possible and thus extend the slaves' days off.

reservations in the land west of Missouri and the transformation of that vast area into Kansas Territory. Eventually, Kansas would enter the Union, and Congress left to its settlers whether Kansas would allow slavery. That decision could affect the split in Congress on the slave issue, so it would have a tremendous effect on national politics. With the whole country looking on, settlers representing both sides poured in to Kansas Territory. Their gateway: a town just incorporated at the riverboat landing on the south bank of the Missouri — the City of Kansas.

A promising start, a raucous celebration

Not even listed in the 1850 census, the City of Kansas was described this way by a settler bound for Kansas Territory who arrived with her family on Nov. 1, 1854:

"After an uneventful voyage of two weeks we landed at Kansas City, Mo., *or rather at a bluff called by that name.*"

Within a few years, Kansas City grew to several thousand residents and surpassed Westport and Independence in population and commercial importance. Its

Christmas Gift!

According to custom, children and servants who cried "Christmas gift!" should get one — if they were fast enough.

One Missouri slave, Malinda Discus, years later recalled how the custom worked: "If we could manage to say 'Christmas gift' to any of the Master's family on Christmas morning before they spoke to us, they would have to give us a gift of some kind. We always mostly were first.

"The gift might be some clothes or a stick of candy. Store candy — as we called it — was a real treat."

Gift giving

Gift giving at year's end has been traced back to Rome, when emperors received gifts from subjects who wanted to show loyalty. Romans also exchanged gifts privately to mark the new year, and often these were of little value.

Not until the 19th century did gift giving become common in the United States. In the early decades, the gift went from higher on the social scale to lower: Adults gave gifts to children, masters to servants.

As the century wore on, the one-way gift process became an exchange, which proved enduringly popular. Gift giving cemented bonds such as family relationships and friendships.

Overindulgence was not frowned on, so even in difficult economic times people went to excess when purchasing gifts for others. The very existence of Christmas became an excuse for spending too much, just as it had long been an excuse for eating and drinking and carousing too much.

Misery on the prairie

As thousands of settlers entered Kansas Territory, a young Methodist preacher from Tennessee in autumn 1855 began organizing congregations. In his travels in east-central Kansas, he faced the privations of life on a treeless prairie, climaxing in one harsh Christmas.

The Rev. Cyrus R. Rice — possessor of a horse, a single suit of clothes and a set of books for religious study — wandered along creeks and rivers in several counties gathering people for services and staying at settlers' homes. Through most of December the weather was mild.

Just before sunset Dec. 22, after Rice arrived at a settler's cabin on Big Sugar Creek in Linn County, the young minister felt a gust of wind from the north. The cabin shook. Rice rushed to help his host bring in wood while "the wind and coldness increased every minute."

The hay that had been stuffed into crevices between the cabin logs began to come out. The north wind roared in, carrying with it snow that covered beds and everything else in the cabin. There was only one place to go — bed.

"We were all in bed, covered 'head and ears,'" Rice recalled. "The snow came down on us all night long. I am sure it was three inches deep on the beds and floor."

Sunday, Dec. 23, was spent not in preaching but in clearing snow out of the cabin and away from the door. Rice and his host family ate one meal, climbed into bed that evening "and just let it snow."

"I drew myself into as small a knot as possible and wished I had never heard of Kansas Territory," he wrote.

About noon on Monday, Christmas eve, the snow ceased, having accumulated "about knee-deep to a horse." As for "cold, uninhabitable Kansas Territory," he said, "I was now sure it never could be settled."

"It was Christmas eve, but we had no merry gathering, no Christmas tree, no plum pudding! We made no effort to have a Merry Christmas. We were in for a cold Christmas."

On the morning of the holiday, Rice left the cabin and made his way across the prairie to Osawatomie.

"There was not much sign of 'Christmas doings' in the town," Rice recalled. "I could not feel any Christmas or New Year's spirit in the cold air. I never heard 'Merry Christmas' or 'Happy New Year' once. The people I met, as well as myself, were not in a merry mood."

aspirations were unbounded.

In 1857 a hundred business leaders were invited to "a magnificent game supper" on Christmas Eve, an event intended to "push on the column of progress." That night, Mayor Milton J. Payne reviewed the city's progress since the opening of Kansas Territory:

"A vast, indeed an almost wonderful change has taken place in our city within the last three years. Hills have been dug away, ravines bridged and filled, streets graded, houses erected, and a general prosperity has been manifested in all branches of trade."

Speaker after speaker hailed the Santa Fe trade, the prosperity of local merchants, the busy real-estate market and the need for a railroad connection to the rest of the country. Cheers were raised, as were many toasts. Toward the end, the celebration was going full-bore, according to an account in *The Journal of Commerce*:

"Mr. Scruggs was then called upon and made some few remarks which the reporter was unable to hear on account of convivial and majestic uproar 'down below.' Mr. Pitkin here made some remarks....He was loudly cheered, but we do not now remember much of the speech."

The racket probably stemmed from perhaps the oldest of all holiday traditions: Drink.

A year later on Christmas eve, the same newspaper noted "several individuals upon the street whose powers of locomotion were greatly in the abstract....They were a little ahead of Christmas license for zig-zag marches and promenades."

Just before that observation was made, the paper reported good-humoredly that a noisy crowd of men and boys had almost come to blows with police at Third and Main streets. It seems that "some of our fellow citizens took time by the forelock and got on a bender before Christmas — the day when benders are in order....They disturbed the peace (that is the English for too much red-eye)." No arrests were made.

Nevertheless, a "Grand Fancy Dress Ball" that drew people from Independence, Westport, Wyandotte City and Kansas City came off without a hitch that same Christmas Eve.

By 1859, the city was staging some even more refined events — a series of "musical soirees," the

The river ices over

"The frost king has sealed up the waters of the Missouri, and erected an impromptu bridge over its turbid channel that is the delight of the juveniles and owners of ice houses..."

— The Enterprise, *Kansas City*, Dec. 20, 1856

1850-1865: STIRRING UP BUSINESS

A holiday mood swing

One of the legion of eastern journalists attracted by the political frenzy in Kansas Territory was George D. Brewerton of the *New York Herald*. On Christmas Day 1855 he was staying at the Shawnee Indian Mission in Johnson County.

"The ground is covered with snow...and for the past three days the mercury here has indicated from 10 to 22 degrees below zero," he wrote. "Siberia itself could hardly look more frigidly repulsive than these frozen, snow-drifted wastes of Eastern Kansas."

Although he was only two miles from Westport and about six miles from Kansas City, Brewerton felt a gloomy isolation.

"There's some mistake this year," he wrote, "for though today is, beyond a doubt, December the 25th, on which...Christmas ought and used to come, we haven't seen it yet — our Christmas we mean.

"Our festival, with its friendly gifts and right good wishes; its turkey dinner, pleased little ones, toasts, mince pie, evergreen-decorated church, sermon and all that sort of thing, is on t'other side of those far-off Allegheny mountains."

That evening, things improved. Thomas Johnson, the

East building of the Indian Mission.

Methodist minister who ran the Indian mission, invited Brewerton to join the family celebration. The reporter's spirits rose. There was a large open fire and several children going through "goodies" that had been placed in their stockings.

"It may interest the New York juveniles," Brewerton wrote, "to know that in the Far Western country, a child's first Christmas salutation to every one it meets is "Christmas gift — Christmas gift."

"They catch you always, if they can. We tried to get ahead of a blue-eyed, curly-headed little lady this morning...but Miss Betty was too smart for us, and cried 'Christmas gift,' before we could open our mouth."

Journal of Commerce said, "an admirable prelude to the Christmas holidays and a source of unalloyed amusement to our citizens."

'Hooray for Christmas!'

As the city grew, so did Christmas retailing.

In the middle 1850s, the news and advertising columns of *The Enterprise*, a weekly newspaper published in Kansas City, made little mention of the word, "Christmas." In December 1856 the paper spoke of a local bookstore with "a splendid assortment of holiday books suitable for children's and new year's presents."

By December 1858 that had changed. Rosser's drugstore in Westport was advertising its line of flavorings — lemon, orange, raspberry, peach, strawberry, vanilla — as "Seasonable: Just in time for

Christmas." A merchant named F. Denzer breathlessly announced his "Children's Christmas market! Just received, exhibited and for sale at the Fruit Room, near the Court House, a large assortment of fancy toys of all descriptions."

One store even had a pre-Christmas sale under way, stating in an advertisement Dec. 21 that it was "desirous of closing out all such goods as are adapted to winter wear only such as blankets, shawls, cloaks and woolen dress goods."

"We are determined to sell the same at reduced prices," said the advertisement of Bruckman & Pulte's on Third Street.

By 1859, Christmas was big business in the area. *The Weekly Border Star* of Westport pointed out: "Christmas is approaching, and our merchants and grocers are getting on their holiday goods. Street & Baker are first in the field with all sorts of fancy groceries and knicknacks."

In mid-December the *Journal of Commerce* outlined the commercial aspect of the season in a way that is instantly recognizable almost a century and a half later:

"From now until after the holidays have passed, very many of

Life on the border

One of the fullest accounts of Christmas on the frontier before the Civil War came from a New England-reared schoolteacher who lived with a family in the countryside along the western border of Missouri. Fanny Hunter, in a book of fiction based on fact, sought to sketch "a picture of the social and moral life" practiced in western Missouri. Her third-person story, *Western Border Life; or What Fanny Hunter Saw and Heard in Kanzas and Missouri*, was published in 1856.

Christmas, she recalled, "was the one jubilee of the year" and Christmas dinner "the one dinner of the year."

"There was no school, but such a succession of dining days, and visiting days, and day parties, and night parties, that Fanny... thought that the regular routine of school duties would be less fatiguing."

Preparations were started days before, and coming from the kitchen were "savory smells of boiled, baked, and roasted meats; and sweet, delicious smells of warm pastry and steaming cakes...The chopping of sausage-meat, the pounding of spices and the beating of eggs was constantly heard.

> 500 lbs. Buffalo Meat,
> New Cider,
> DRESSED POULTRY,
> Potatoes, Turnips, Beets,
> With a general assortment of
> STAPLE & FANCY GROCERIES,
> SUITABLE FOR THE HOLIDAYS,
> Received and for sale by
> LYONS,
> Main Street, opposite Odd Fellows' Hall.

From the *Journal of Commerce*, Dec. 24, 1858.

"Christmas morning came, and, long before daylight, every child upon the place, both black and white, was up ready to 'march in Christmas.'"

This was a parade of noise. Horns blowing, cowbell ringing, hands clapping, tin pans being beaten with sticks, the children entered the house and marched up the stairs to the sleeping rooms of adults. Having awakened anyone still snoozing in the main house, the diverse set of marchers headed back to the slave cabins to repeat the clamorous performance.

The Christmas dance was at the home of a neighboring farmer. According to custom, Hunter reported, the partygoers spent the night, so servants were recruited to carry carpet bags and valises containing party dresses.

1850-1865: STIRRING UP BUSINESS

Food

"Fresh and nice oysters can be bought cheap at the Express office. Now is the time to secure something extra for Christmas — something for an oyster pie, or oyster dressing for the big Christmas turkey."

— *Journal of Commerce,* Dec. 22, 1858.

"We are to have some fine beef for Christmas. We noticed yesterday Mr. Kelly and Mr. Mason driving three of the largest and fattest stall-fed steers through Main Street that we ever saw in possession of a Kansas City butcher. The cattle were raised and fattened in Clay County and are a credit to the farmer, whoever he may be, who raised them."

— *Journal of Commerce,* Dec. 23, 1858

"We were surprised yesterday to see such a variety of the solid and substantial Christmas dinner eatables in our market. Everybody we met had a basket containing more or less of these solids — oysters, turkeys, chickens, geese, rabbits, squirrels, quails, fish, ducks, wild turkey, prairie chickens, buffalo meat, venison, opposum, snipe and a great variety of other fixings. If anybody in this city has much of an appetite after four o'clock tomorrow, we shall be greatly mistaken."

— *Journal of Commerce,* Dec. 24, 1859

Nellie McCoy Harris, daughter of one of Kansas City's founders, John Calvin McCoy, recalled early festivities among the growing city's upper crust. The family of A.B.H. McGee, she wrote decades later in *The Kansas City Times*, was "lavish to extravagance in the supply of good things at their feasts."

"Turkeys and hams, chickens, roast pig, saddle of mutton, and sometimes venison and buffalo were served. In the center of each table was placed a large stack of pyramid cake, and sometimes one at each end."

Drink

A Southerner who came to Kansas Territory in support of slavery, A.J. Hoole told how he spent Christmas 1856.

Learning that there was to be a meeting of pro-slavery settlers, Hoole dropped his plan to hunt squirrels and joined a gathering of 12 to 15 men. One of them "endeavored to explain the object" of the meeting, and endeavored, and endeavored — perhaps a half-dozen times. After two hours of listening to the verbal stumbling, Hoole wrote, "I gathered enough to find out that it was to appoint a delegate to the pro-slavery convention.

"The speaker was drunk.

"They had four bottles of liquor, and before the meeting broke up (for it did not adjourn) one got so drunk that he fell down; another got about a hundred yards off, and there he lay. Others got pretty boozy, but they kept their feet. At least they were up when I left.

"Thus passed my Christmas."

* * *

In late December 1859, the editor of the short-lived *Border Star* of Westport related a Christmas dream in which one vision showed "an army of inebriate youths celebrating in revelry the advent of the Savior and at the same time forcibly illustrating their great need of salvation."

Another article in the same issue reported a fire that broke out at noon Christmas Day, destroying many stores and homes in Westport. In all the commotion, the newspaper said, "A great deal of free liquor was rolled out into the street, and a great many free drinkers took advantage of it. They got a cheap Christmas spree."

* * *

"We do intend to do one thing...namely, to take a sufficient quantity of hens' eggs, to beat the yolks and whip the whites, to mix a modicum of white sugar, and mingle a quantity of good old rye or bourbon, to refrain from all approach to water as persistently as a mad dog, and then mix all these together in a large white bowl, with a large white ladle, and then we intend to invite (others) to test the quality of our manufacture; and then we intend to test it again; and then to do so once more; and then we intend to test it several times, until, we...give vent to our enthusiasm by wishing ten thousand merry Christmases to every man, woman and child in the Centropolis of the Universe!"

— *Journal of Commerce*,
Dec. 24, 1859

* * *

"A very large article of 'big drunk' came over a portion of our community, involving many who 'never did the like' before; but then you know it was Christmas. Whether or not any carnival, like of old Rome, will continue seven days, we would not dare predict."

— *Journal of Commerce*,
Dec. 27, 1860.

1850-1865: STIRRING UP BUSINESS

our business houses will have some special advertisements....Toy dealers, booksellers confectionists, fruit dealers, milliners, etc. etc. always make extra preparation for the holidays and for weeks previous to the advent of old Santa Claus we have been accustomed to see the shop windows filled with everything attractive...The retail trade for the next three weeks...will be worth more than any six weeks of the fall and winter season."

Christmas 1860 was a carnival, according to the *Journal of Commerce*:

"Hooray for Christmas!...We doubt if ever such a Christmas day was seen in Kansas City. The ladies went to the festival, to the balls and went sleighing. The young men sleighed and *slewed*: eggnog, nothing but eggnog, being the prevailing sentiments of the day. The old folks enjoyed their turkey dinners and social chats, the little folks reveled in confectionaries and the juveniles fired their crackers and charged down the hills upon their sleds."

Several days of snowfall had made the ground perfect for sleighs, an uncommon event at Christmastime.

"Christmas only comes once a year, and sleighing snows once in five," the *Journal of Commerce* said, "so let her slide."

So much in a holiday mood was the newspaper that it published, evidently for the first time, "A Visit From St. Nicholas" attributed to Clement C. Moore.

On Christmas Eve 1860, outside the Presbyterian Ladies Festival on Main Street, two male friends got into an argument "in a moment of excitement, while under the influence of a little spree they were having." One struck the other and the other shot the first in the leg. No charges were expected.

Business was booming, at Christmas time and also throughout the year. But the very cause of the boom, the opening of Kansas Territory, was about to lie at the heart of a resounding bust.

War and bust

Kansas finally was admitted to the Union in 1861, its constitution banning slavery. The Union,

Toys of the times: A china head doll, made about 1860.

CHRISTMASTIME IN KANSAS CITY

meanwhile, split in two. The Kansas-Missouri border became a flashpoint.

Kansas City's position at the nexus of the slavery struggle, recently a boon to its commerce, now isolated the town. A force of Union soldiers dispatched from Fort Leavenworth occupied the city, where residents' sympathies were split. The territory around it was continually consumed in guerrilla warfare. The countryside was occupied by bands of armed men who claimed to be with the Union or with the Confederacy, but who often resembled little more than hoodlums.

The perilous times were reflected in an incident that occurred on Christmas 1861. That day there was to be a dance at Westport for young women and for young men who were not in the army of one side or another. Decades after the war, Mrs. W. A. Mahaffey of Olathe recalled what happened:

At the height of the merriment, a company of guerrillas "in the service of William C. Quantrill" burst in. One guerrilla, Mrs. Mahaffey said, wore the topcoat of a Union officer who had been captured in a skirmish. Blood was visible on the collar.

The guerrillas danced through the evening with the hoop-skirted women, who did not have a choice. Then as swiftly as they arrived the guerrillas mounted their horses and rode away.

By 1863, the Civil War had made its impression on commerce. Louis Denzer's store, according to the *Journal of Commerce*, would have for sale to Christmas shoppers Union flags and Union lanterns in addition to "firecrackers, torpedoes and all other kinds of fireworks."

The war apparently had not entirely dampened spirits. According to the newspaper, "Today all Christendom indulges in unbridled festivities. The world is one long, wild, harum-scarum holiday and life a grand frolic, set round with tin trumpets and rattles."

Yet danger was not far distant. Some Union scouts brought into Kansas City two men they found in suspicious circumstance the day after

"Hooray for Christmas!...We doubt if ever such a Christmas day was seen in Kansas City. The ladies went to the festival, to the balls and went sleighing."

— Journal of Commerce, *Dec. 27, 1860*

1850-1865: STIRRING UP BUSINESS

Christmas near Sni-a-Bar Creek. On the same day, three companies of the 15th Kansas were reported to have arrived in town.

By Christmas 1864, there was less evidence of good feeling and merriment. Only two months before, the area had survived a battle between an army of Confederate raiders and Union troops. In the three-day Battle of Westport from Oct. 21 to Oct. 23, about 3,500 men were killed or severely wounded.

When the main forces of the Confederacy surrendered in Virginia the following spring, Kansas City was struggling. Years of guerrilla activity in the countryside, months of threatened military attack and finally a serious engagement at the city's doorstep — the Battle of Westport — had crippled commerce. On Christmas Eve, only a single wagon-load of turkeys was spotted in town, and they were going for as much as $2.50 — roughly $25 in today's money.

"Poor man's turkeys," a newspaper said, "are decidedly scarce."

And the end of the war did not bring an end to animosity. On Christmas night 1865, at a dance in Lee's Summit, several U.S. soldiers argued with bushwhackers over dancing partners. On the street outside a fight broke out and shots were fired. A passenger train going through town on the Missouri Pacific railroad was fired into. Only one injury was reported.

Even so, by that same Christmas the area was feeling a sense of relief that the war was over.

"A year ago on Christmas night our citizens had to report for detail upon 'guard duty,' " the *Journal of Commerce* noted. "But this time 'Merry Christmas' was the countersign and everybody seemed to know it."

Things to come: Only four years after the Civil War ended, Kansas City would get the commercial boost it had long dreamed of — a new bridge to carry railroad trains across the Missouri River and on to eastern markets. This panoramic map depicted the city in 1869, when the bridge opened.

3 | 1866-1890
Hustle and bustle

By the end of the 1860s, the city that limped out of the Civil War found itself healthy, prosperous and trading with the world. The reason was the new Kansas City bridge, the first permanent structure to carry rails across the Missouri River.

Once construction of the bridge was completed in 1869, trains connected Kansas City with the markets of Chicago and the East. Packinghouses and grain elevators, warehouses and roundhouses sprang up where the tracks emptied into the West Bottoms. The city's working class exploded in number, and the city's elite grew in size and in wealth. Total population would rocket past 20,000 in 1870, even by estimates more conservative than the U.S. census.

Unlike the frontier outpost of 4,000 of pre-war days, Kansas City now had a wealth of Christmas entertainments. At the Good Templar's festival on Dec. 23, 1869, a promenade concert was followed by recitations, songs, violin solos, a grand march, and then supper and dancing. On Christmas Eve there was a dance at the Broadway Hotel, admission $5 a person. The City Market stayed open until 8 p.m. that day for last-minute grocery shoppers.

For children, the Grand Avenue Methodist church promised a free Christmas Eve program, including an appearance by Santa Claus. Christmas night at the same church, admission was 25 cents to a musical festival to benefit the Kansas City Mission Sunday School. A Christmas dinner was staged by the former pastor of the black Baptist church on Christmas day, featuring turkey, chicken, pheasant, quail, beef, venison, buffalo, rabbit and pork as the meat dishes.

On this first Christmas after the opening of the bridge, "rockets at intervals went up," *The Kansas City Times* reported. "The city was jubilant with songs and laughter. The city had put on holiday attire."

Christmas all around

The new bridge not only delivered Kansas City's products to the rest of the

One of a series of colorful Christmas advertisements carried on a card by Nicolai & Michaelis, whose store was listed at this address in the early 1880s.

Christmas trees

Like the legend of Santa Claus, the popularity of the Christmas tree grew rapidly in the 19th century. The tree was a German custom imported to the New World by people of German ancestry. Its use was limited, however, until the 1830s, when it began to appear in literature. Simultaneously, magazines, newspapers and books were growing in distribution and affordability. The popularity of trees spread rapidly.

The Christmas tree was an attractive icon of the season. Decorated with candles, it brought light, colorful decorations and a bit of green nature indoors during a dark and gray time of year.

An early instance of the custom west of the Mississippi River occurred in 1833. On Christmas Day that year Gustave Koerner, of German descent, paid a visit to a St. Louis friend, George Engelmann. The two made a "kind of pedestal" from a small sassafras tree that still bore some leaves. In his *Memoirs*, Koerner recalled that the children of the house had "dressed the tree with ribbons and bits of colored paper and the like, had put wax candles on the branches, and had hung it with little red apples and nuts and all sorts of confectionery."

In 1850, the nationally circulated magazine *Godey's Lady's Book* published an illustration of a decorated evergreen surrounded by a family. By 1869, according to the *Annals of Platte County*, Christmas trees were becoming common in western Missouri. By the 1870s churches had Christmas trees, both in the city and the country.

In the 1920s, an 83-year-old German-born carpenter told a reporter for *The Kansas City Star* that he had erected the first lighted tree in Westport. The event took place at the home of Oswald Karl Lux on Archibald Street in 1882, the family's second Christmas in the United States.

Recalling trees in his native country, Lux tried to find a suitable one here, but none was taller than 18 inches nor strong enough to carry toys, sweets or candles. He fashioned his own branches from the staves of a nail keg, attached them to a broomstick, wrapped the wood in red paper, tipped the "branches" with silver paper and covered the artificial tree with evergreen sprigs from Union Cemetery.

Lux nailed small, fat candles to each "branch" and lighted the whole affair on Christmas morning, bringing joy not only to his three daughters but also to neighbor children who saw the tree through a window.

That same year, a vice president of Edison Electric in New York, whose neighborhood was the first in New York City to have electricity, claimed to have been the first to add electric lights to his tree. Small bulbs were hand-blown and hand-wired in the company laboratory.

In Kansas city, another electric company executive led the way. Edwin R. Weeks, who built Kansas City's first electric plant as manager of the Kawsmouth Electric Co. in 1881, was said to have had the first electric Christmas tree lights. They were installed sometime in the late 1800s on a tree in the bay window of his home at 1409 Cherry St.

Cause and effect?

"Dec. 24 (1869) — Christmas trees everywhere. W.E. Stitt's house, fully insured, burned."

— *Annals of Platte County*

country, it also brought the rest of the country's merchandise to Kansas City. Mass production of goods surged after the Civil War in the industrial Northeast, and the spread of railroads nationwide created markets for those products.

After the bridge opened, Kansas City retailing boomed. That was obvious at Christmastime.

E. Jaccard & Co. at 613 Main St. boasted in 1869 that it had the finest assortment of holiday goods ever brought to the city: chains, bracelets, mantle clocks and so on. By Christmas Eve 1871, merchants were promoting jewelry, stationery, silver plate, solid silver, watches, diamonds, albums — even sewing machines.

The season already was growing longer. In 1871, Matt, Foster & Co. advertised as early as Nov. 26 that the holidays were coming and the company was "thoroughly prepared to supply an unlimited number of customers....Give them an early call." On Nov. 24, 1875, Long & Haag was advertising "Toys, toys, toys at wholesale prices." The merchants said they were going out of business at year's end, making this "your time to select and buy your toys for the

1866-1890: HUSTLE AND BUSTLE

Noise and sparks

"While firing a Roman candle last night to celebrate Christmas, Master Willie Sawyer, a young lad whose father lives in the addition, had his face very badly burnt and one eye seriously injured by a premature explosion."

— The Kansas City Times, *Dec. 27, 1869*

"Chinese crackers were quite numerous last evening, and the popping and snapping made by the noisy little things gave evidence that Christmas was not far away....

"The atmosphere was resonant with the toot of many horns. There were many other horns which were not heard, simply because it wasn't safe for those who had them to play too loud."

— Journal of Commerce, *Dec. 25, 1875*

"Some small boys were making lots of noise all day long by firing off a small-sized cannon on the Public Square.

"A slightly inebriated granger amused himself and about a dozen boot blacks by setting fire to a half-dozen packs of Chinese crackers in front of the Barnum House about dusk."

— The Times, *Dec. 26, 1875*

In Independence, "the usual dangerous and mischievous practice of letting off firecrackers and pistols in the public streets yesterday was freely indulged in, causing considerable scare and annoyance to pedestrians and horses."

— The Times, *Dec. 26, 1875*

holidays."

On Dec. 3, 1875, the Diamond Tea Store acknowledged the existence of public frustration at early-season ads:

"Don't talk of Christmas yet," I think I
hear you say;
"Postpone the subject 'till a later day."

But in the same verse replied:

"One month will soon slip round; too
soon alas!
A week or two will very quickly pass;
And, mark! unless we look at our
affairs
The approaching time will take us
unawares.
Is it too early to begin to save?
No! Not if you your Christmas
comforts crave..."

Toys for children were advertised in growing variety and complexity. John Doggett's 1875 stock included toy steam engines, printing presses, bows and arrows, "and thousands of other popular toys which are sure to delight the children at Christmas and for months after."

For adults, meanwhile, Bullene, Moore & Emerys had inlaid writing desks; bronze urns, stands, pitchers, paperweights and thermometers; pearl, ivory and carved-handle fans; men's silk and cashmere mufflers, and white and fancy-bordered silk handkerchiefs.

Bullene promised a dazzling display with "every available place crowded with holiday goods," and even a social occasion: "Ladies will meet all of their friends this week in Bullene, Moore & Emerys' Beautiful Temple Store."

Dazzle became competitive. As Christmas neared in 1875, Cady & Olmsteads jewelers produced a "grand illumination" several nights in a row by lighting "a thousand gas jets."

Out in the Johnson County countryside, meanwhile, John B. White's Emporium Store of Olathe was marking down his boots and shoes to actual cost — for cash customers — and also offering these holiday presents:

■ Ladies' cardigan jackets

■ Linen handkerchiefs, "put up in nice boxes of a half-dozen lots, fragrantly scented with musk, (Those desiring camphor can have it)."

■ "Nice line of gents' handkerchiefs....Any young lady

The approach of Christmas, 1871

"Sleigh-bells ringing...

All sorts of sleighs go out...

Six inebriates arrested last night.

The streets were crowded yesterday...

Christmas presents were being sold at all the stores last night...

A drunken women brought to jail last night on a wheelbarrow...

Several accidents to sleighing parties occurred yesterday...

There is a suggestion of mince meat and turkey in the air...

People began celebrating last night. The streets were animated until after midnight."

— *Brief reports from* The Kansas City Times, *Dec. 24, 1871*

1866-1890: HUSTLE AND BUSTLE

In the churches

On Christmas night 1875 the packed house for services at Second Presbyterian Church, Eighth and Wyandotte streets, found the tree next to the pulpit lighted with candles and laden with presents. "Without the evergreen in church or school room, Christmas would seem a solemn occasion," the *Journal of Commerce* wrote of the occasion.

Santa Claus, "his grotesque dress and odd actions provoking laughter," according to the *Journal*, appeared at the Third, or West Kansas, Presbyterian Church at 13th and Hickory streets in the West Bottoms.

The first service held at the new St. Patricks' Roman Catholic Church, Eighth and Cherry streets, was high Mass on Christmas Day 1875. The brand new building was unfinished inside and participants had temporary seating. Nevertheless, Haydn's Second Mass in C was brought off well, according to *The Times*.

By 1880, a long list of churches in Wyandotte City — the heart of what would become Kansas City, Kan., in 1886 — boasted Christmas trees. Among them were Methodist,

St. Patrick's church

Episcopal, Presbyterian and African Methodist Episcopal, not to mention various churches in Rosedale and west of state line in the West Bottoms.

buying a box of handkerchiefs for a present will get a cake of fine soap thrown in as an inducement for the young gentleman who receives the present to keep a clean face and hands."

On Christmas Day 1875, businesses in Kansas City were open early and closed by noon.

Some people walked the streets in groups, staring into show windows, and others attended the matinee at the Coates Opera House, a comic opera performance. Still others rode horseback or drove carriages around town.

Hotels such as the Pacific, St. James and Lindell near the City Market, the Coates on Broadway and the Leland on Union Avenue were open for Christmas dinner.

Other precincts were not so genteel. The police reported more drunkenness and "riotous behavior" than in any 24 hours of the preceding 12 months.

"Many an individual who started out in the morning with good resolutions," *The Times* reported, "found himself in the lockup before night."

Early Christmas afternoon, for example, a man "very badly afflicted

Tummy aches

On Christmas Eve, 1880, *The Times* printed this poem, parodying "A Visit from St. Nicholas."

'Twas the night after Christmas, when all through the house
Every soul was abed, and as still as a mouse;
Those stockings so lately St. Nicholas' care,
Were emptied of all that was eatable there;
The darlings had duly been tucked in their beds,
With very full stomachs and pains in their heads.

I was dozing away in my new cotton cap,
And Nannie was rather far gone in a nap,
When out of the nursery arose such a clatter,
I sprang from my sleep, crying, "What is the matter?"
I flew to their bedside — still half in a doze,
Tore open the curtains and threw off the clothes,
While the light of the taper served clearly to show
The piteous plight of those objects below,
For what to the fond father's eyes should appear
But the little pale face of each sick little dear,
For each pet that had crammed itself full as a tick,
I knew in a moment now felt like old Nick.

At this point, the author accedes to his wife's suggestion that a doctor be called. The doctor arrives in his carriage, evidently inebriated.

He was covered with mud from his head to his foot,
And the suit he had on was the very worst suit;
And he hardly had time to put that on his back,
And he look'd like Falstaff half fuddled with sack,
His eyes, how they twinkled! Had the Doctor got merry?
His cheeks looked like port and his breath smelt of sherry....

Nevertheless, the doctor "physicks" the children, leaves directions and returns to his horsedrawn vehicle.

Then he jumped in his gig — gave old Jalap a whistle,
And Jalap dashed off as if pricked by a thistle.
But the Doctor exclaimed ere he drove out of sight,
"They'll be well by tomorrow — good night! Jones — good night!"

Was the author of this rather skillfully done parody Eugene Field, then editor of *The Times*, and later to win fame as the Hoosier poet?

with bad whisky" rammed his arm through a saloon window at Broadway and Fifth streets, breaking the window and badly cutting himself. Drunkenness as a Christmas tradition remained firmly in place.

Yet other traditions were in place, too, most of them more benign. This poem of the middle 1870s mentions many Christmas icons that remained familiar a century later:

"Come, lay aside your work-day care,
And bring free hearts along.
The while we tell a pleasant tale
And sing a Christmas song;

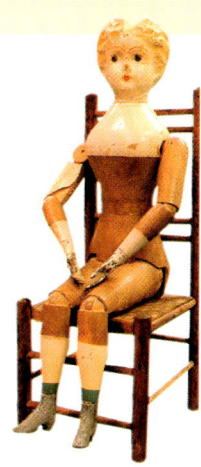

Toys of the times: This doll was manufactured about 1880.

1866-1890: HUSTLE AND BUSTLE

Our tale's of merry men and times.
Our song a song of cheer;
And then we'll to our evening joys
For Christmas now is here.

"We'll deck the walls with ivy green,
With holly ripe and red.
Till on the air a soft perfume
From Christmas-boughs is shed;
Then we'll invoke good Santa Claus
Well laden to appear,
And hold each spray, each stocking fill,
For Christmas now is here.

"We'll spread the cloth and fill the board,
Our choicest vintage bring,
And mirth and laughter through the halls
In joyous shouts shall ring;
Our glasses tip in social glee
Which friends to friends endear.
And pledge each other merrily,
For Christmas now is here.

"Then to music's witching strains,
In mirth and dance and song,
With hearts as light as snow-flakes bring
We'll pass the hours along;
And when our revels all are past,
And dies the waning year,
We'll hope for many other days
Of merry Christmas here."

— The Times, *Dec. 25, 1876*

In four stanzas, the poet evoked a day off work, carols, ivy, holly, the tree, Santa, stockings, presents, a banquet, strong drink, jollity, get-togethers with friends, snowflakes and nostalgia.

More strong drink

"Seeing a lamp post leaning up against a man last evening reminded us that yesterday was Christmas.

"We risk nothing in asserting that headache prevails to an alarming extent among the menfolk of Kansas City this morning."

— The Kansas City Times, *Dec. 26, 1880.*

"'Twas Christmas broached the mightiest ale;
'Twas Christmas told the merriest tale;
A Christmas gambol oft would cheer
A poor man's heart through half the year.

"It was probably from this old English song that the young man of the period got his authority for celebrating Christmas by looking up the 'mightiest ale' available. From the indications on the streets last night he found some of the mightiest ever broached on Christmas eve. There is no orthodox origin for the Christmas drunk, but it has grown to be one of the most popular forms of observations among certain classes."

— The Kansas City Star, *Dec. 25, 1885*

The big time

The 1880s saw the Kansas City area's greatest percentage growth ever. Kansas City would jump from almost 56,000 residents to more than 132,000. Kansas City, Kan., consolidated from several Wyandotte County towns in 1886, would have more than 54,000 residents by the end of the decade.

Eastern money was pouring in to the area real-estate market. Impressive buildings such as the New York Life Building and the New England Building were rising on Ninth Street. The government built a big new post office, customs house and federal courts building at Ninth and Walnut streets. The city was paving streets. The Board of Trade constructed an architectural treasure on Eighth Street, and Bullene, Moore, Emery was preparing to move to a massive new structure on 11th Street between Walnut Street and Grand Avenue.

Christmas sales shot through the roof. On Christmas Eve 1885 merchants reported the largest trade

To a child's eyes

"As children we all knew the spell of this season. We used to count the days which yet remained before Christmas would come. We all used to believe in the pleasant myth of *Santa Claus*. We looked in the fresh fallen snow for the tracks of his reindeer, without success, and we looked in the stockings by the fireplace for evidence of his visit, with good success....

"Because the children love it, because the poor love it, as well as and even more than because of its other pleasures and enhancements it is good to observe this Christmas Day."

— *Editorial in* The Star, *Dec. 24, 1885.*

Growing up fast: Downtown Kansas City in 1888, as depicted in *Harper's Illustrated*.

1866-1890: HUSTLE AND BUSTLE

Christmas cards

Christmas greeting cards were introduced to the United States on a large scale in the mid-1870s by German-born Louis Prang of Boston, who since the Civil War had manufactured business cards, announcements and advertisements. His finely printed, colorful cards made large profits and dominated the market until competitors found cheaper ways to make and sell greeting cards in the 1890s.

The expanding rail network made postal service faster and more reliable and so Christmas greeting cards proliferated among Americans, who were more mobile and thus spread farther apart as each decade passed.

"For the large body of people who desire to send to their friends some slight token of continued remembrance and regard at the Christmastide," *The Star* wrote in 1885, "Christmas cards have become a recognized institution.... While low in price they are not cheap in estimation."

They also were easier to send than traditional letters, could replace the old Christmas tradition of making personal holiday visits to acquaintances and could even substitute for gifts.

Louis Prang cards

CHRISTMASTIME IN KANSAS CITY

in the city's history. They credited spending by the working class, newly prosperous as a result of jobs created by all the construction and public improvements. These jobs were plentiful even in winter.

"The stores look as though they have been struck by a cyclone," *The Kansas City Star* wrote. "The enormous stocks which were displayed to such advantage a few weeks ago are nothing but confused wrecks composed of odds and ends."

At Union Depot in the West Bottoms, the waiting rooms were packed with people from the countryside who had come to the city to buy presents. The depot was a happy place for pickpockets, too. In the week before Christmas 1885, they arrived early each morning, worked the crowds for money and disappeared until the next day. One man lost $100 — equal to more than $1,500 in 2001 currency.

By 1890 the crush at Union Depot was nearly unbearable. Long waits for tickets meant some travelers missed their trains and had to wait until evening to return home. Railroads begin considering construction of a new station. The post office, meanwhile, faced its busiest day in history that year, with customers sending packages and buying stamps and money orders.

"The custom of making Christmas presents is so general and religiously adhered to," *The Kansas City Star* remarked, "that one can scarcely find a family unless homeless, penniless and friendless, whose home is not brightened on Christmas by happy faces bending above gifts from 'Santa Claus.'"

Children hung their stockings, top, and later Santa warmed his hands by the fire in these advertising cards by Nicolai & Michaelis.

40 CHRISTMASTIME IN KANSAS CITY

Rich and poor

Yet in Kansas City, as across the country, the gulf was growing between the well-off who could afford a pleasant Christmas and those people who were "homeless, penniless and friendless." There also existed thousands of Kansas Citians only slightly better off, whose homes were tumbledown shacks hard by the stockyards and packinghouses and surrounded by their smoke and stench. Their paychecks were not enough to afford shoes for their children.

Among some American ministers, a movement had developed called the Social Gospel, a reform effort that applied biblical principles such as charity and justice to the problems of the poor. Eventually, the movement would lead to legal solutions such as the abolition of child labor, shortened workweeks and factory regulation.

More immediately, the Social Gospel aimed to promote charity, private giving meant to soften the conditions of poverty. In the Christmas season, the movement would find the perfect occasion for its work. In Kansas City, it would find a solid corps of adherents.

Blessing the meek

"In such cold weather as this, when the cold pinches and frost hits, the poor and unfortunate should be remembered."

— Journal of Commerce, *Dec. 18, 1863*

"A stranger entered the pavilion of the Widows' and Orphans' home last night and handed Miss Roberts $5 for the most worthy object of charity in the city. The lady had heard Mrs. Holmes speaking of a family in destitute circumstances, and gave the money to her for their relief, and doubtless today glad hearts bless the generosity of the unknown donor."

— The Times, *Dec. 25, 1870*

In response to a resident overheard wishing that there was no Christmas ("A waste of time that encouraged the young people to acts of vanity"), a *Times* writer on Christmas Day 1876 described this scene set in "a certain little cabin in Hell's half-acre":

"Two ladies, warmly wrapped, standing over a pale, emaciated boy, unloading a Christmas basket at his bedside — while his mother and crippled brother stand by and bless Him in whose name Christmas was founded. This was only one instance noticed during the snowstorm yesterday, but it was one of the many silent acts performed in the name of Christmas, and yet there are those who dare to grumble because Christmas comes."

4 | 1890-1918
A season for charity

The day: Christmas 1895. The scene: City Hall, Fourth and Main Streets. The mayor was about to feed Kansas City's newsboys and bootblacks.

About noon they began arriving, packing the fourth floor of City Hall, boys and young men, "black, white and yellow, Jew and Gentile," *The Kansas City Times* reported. Many of these streetwise entrepreneurs were orphans, and all were poor. First, they had to wash up. No dirty hands, no dirty faces were allowed. The "king of the newsboys," Dave Harvey, had a towel and a club to make sure the rules were followed.

His Honor, Mayor Webster Davis, arrived amid cheers. He distributed tin horns among the 250-odd participants. Then the assemblage rushed downstairs, formed a crude line and — amid blaring horns, shouts, more cheers and with a tattered U.S. flag from a nearby saloon at the fore — marched off to dinner. The destination was Staley & Dunlap's Restaurant five blocks south.

More than once in 1895, Kansas City's Haves took the occasion of Christmastime to feed, clothe and reward Have-nots. By the 1890s charitable events like this were common in many parts of the United States, well-subscribed and much-noticed.

Sometimes their sponsors were wealthy attention-seekers and politicians seeking popularity and votes. Cynics saw such once-a-year displays of

Above: This postcard-style Christmas greeting was sent from Germany to a Kansas City resident early in the 20th century. The greeting translates to "Joyous Christmas." Right: Poor people awaited the distribution of baskets by the Salvation Army on Christmas Day 1905.

1890-1918: A SEASON FOR CHARITY

The carol philosophy

The charitable ideal was most memorably expressed in Charles Dickens' *A Christmas Carol*.

The story was written in 1842 and became an instant hit, first in Britain and, by the 1860s, in the United States. Dickens toured the East Coast in 1867, giving readings before large crowds.

As the plot of *A Christmas Carol* unfolds, the primary character, Ebenezer Scrooge, scorns all requests for donations to help the poor. A long nightmare, however, shows him the error of his ways. Scrooge awakens on Christmas Day redeemed, gives freely of his fortune to help others and winds up a beloved man.

A Christmas Carol was a paean to the goodness of private charity, even if the charity was limited to a certain time of the year. Charity brought some balance against the acquisitiveness of the age. Thus was born the "carol philosophy," an attack on selfishness and greed, and an appeal to brotherhood and generosity.

This card, produced in Great Britain, was sent from Kearney in Clay County to Liberty in 1912.

generosity as a way for the wealthy or powerful not only to relieve some guilt, but also to receive a rare display of gratitude.

Yet true altruists were involved, too — not all of them wealthy or powerful. Many altruists were adherents of the Social Gospel movement, which stressed human beings' obligations to one another. Such sentiments could express themselves as nothing more than cheerful greetings to passersby. Or they could become the basis for charity; thousands of people, rich and not so rich, could participate.

Whatever the motive, doing good for the less fortunate fitted perfectly into the ideal of Christmas.

'Eat, boys and girls, eat'

In the late 19th century — the Gilded Age — the wealthy were few, the middle class was only beginning to grow in proportion and the poor were vast in number. By the mid-1890s, a farm crisis of several year's duration, compounded by the national financial panic of 1893, had crimped the lives of many in the Kansas City area and brought desolation to the poorest. Government welfare programs lay years away.

Relieving poverty permanently was too big a task. Staging a Christmastime event to feed, house or clothe the poor was more realistic.

Some of the wealthy poured great effort into these benefactions. In Kansas City's West Bottoms in 1895, railroad baron Arthur E. Stilwell put on a supper and Christmas-tree gift-giving for children of the poor neighborhood. They were students at Bethany night school, which Stilwell had established with his own money to teach standard lessons and also to

The Christmas economy

Turn-of-the-century retailers advertised extravagantly with long lists of goods and prices, and large graphics to attract customers. Newspaper advertisements were effusive in offering men's, women's and children's clothing; whiskey and wine; cigars; pianos and sheet music; toys; groceries; candy — even steel kitchen ranges.

1890

1890

1890

1890

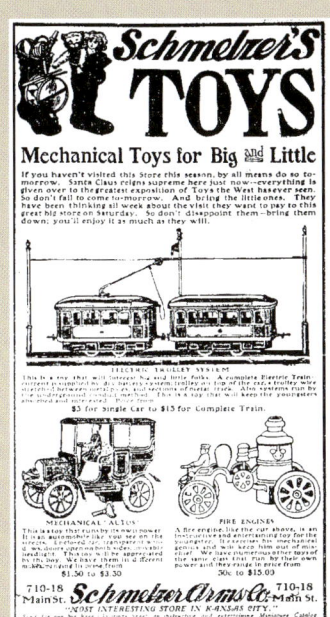
1907

1907

CHRISTMASTIME IN KANSAS CITY

1890-1918: A SEASON FOR CHARITY

A turn-of-the century Christmas dinner gathering.

promote Christian Science.

The 100 or so boys and girls at the supper sang hymns, opened favors and then dived into dinner. Oranges, rarely seen in that poverty-stricken neighborhood, were gobbled up first.

"Eat, boys and girls, eat," Stilwell said as he walked among the diners. "See how much you can eat."

At the mayor's feast that same year, the newsboys and bootblacks needed no encouragement. They composed a conspicuous segment of the poor; their work demanded that they spend a lot of time on the streets, vigorously and vociferously competing with others. The phalanx of these who heeded the mayor's call on Christmas afternoon 1895 poured into Staley & Dunlap's, as one observer said, like a tidal wave. In minutes the tables were full and the patrons demanding to be served. On the menu were roast turkey with cranberry sauce, roast beef, potato salad, mashed potatoes, corn, peas, ice cream, cake, coffee, milk, bread, butter and pickles.

The usual order, *The Times* reported, was "Gimme de hull bizness."

Cheers greeted the arrival of ice cream. Cheers greeted speeches by the mayor and by Harvey, "king of the newsboys." Cheers erupted after grace. Cheers were raised even for a photographer's flash.

By 4 p.m., the feast was over and the participants scattered, each carrying a free box of candy. The event was paid out of the mayor's funds and from the pocketbooks of a few wealthy sympathizers.

A larger set of contributors pitched in for another mayoral event, the Mayor's Christmas fund. In fact, Christmas 1895 ended a long and busy week for Mayor Davis. That morning he had been at City Hall overseeing distribution of the last of more than 1,200 baskets of food bought with contributions to the fund.

Wrap it!

Gift-wrapping became a seasonal routine in the 1880s, adding an element of sweet secrecy and eventual surprise to the exchange. This was the Victorian Era, which called for covering almost everything in sight with something else — from covering floors with rugs to furniture with antimacassars.

Until the late 1910s, however, wrapping material typically was paper or tissue of a single color — white, red or green — or paper or cardboard boxes printed in a holly motif. That changed in the late 1910s, in downtown Kansas City, at a card shop on 11th Street run by Joyce Hall and his brothers. As Hall remembered it, the store sold out of the standard wrapping papers. His brother Rollie Hall combed the Halls' plant and found some large envelope linings printed with fancy patterns that had been imported from France. The Halls sold these for 10 cents a sheet, and they proved exceedingly popular. Within two years, the company added to its burgeoning greeting-card business the manufacture of wrapping paper. Soon, the Halls were producing gift-wrapping kits with paper, tags and ribbon in attractive combinations.

Safer trees

Electric lights for Christmas trees appeared on the American market in 1901, introduced by General Electric. Battery-powered versions were available in the early 1900s for homes without electricity.

Their introduction came none too soon. All too common were incidents like this one, which occurred in Kansas City on Christmas Eve 1905.

About 7 p.m., J.T. Esmond, dressed in Santa Claus costume with a sack of toys, made a grand entrance at the home of relatives on Locust Street. There, family members were gathered around a tree trimmed with popcorn, tinsel and lighted candles. Esmond, seeing one candle not burning, leaned over to light it. His costume caught fire. The flames spread to his pack of toys, and then to curtains at a window near the tree. As some relatives fought the fire, Esmond's wife rushed to the fire station a block away.

Firefighters extinguished the blaze in minutes, but Esmond was burned on the head, arms and hands — wounds later described as painful but not serious. Two women in the home were burned slightly, their hair singed.

"Never again for me; someone else will have to play Santa Claus next year," Esmond said.

A few blocks west that same year, at 18th and Central streets, a teenage girl was burned while battling a tree set on fire by an oil lamp.

Across the United States by 1920, electric lights had replaced candles on most trees.

A Christmas tree in 1897, lighted apparently by candles.

Baskets and banquets

The Social Gospel also generated broad support for agencies like the Salvation Army. Among the Army's efforts was an annual Christmas-Day dinner staged in cities nationwide. In Kansas City in 1895, contributions were enough to feed 750 persons, mostly men, at the Salvation Army installation on Walnut Street. The recipients ate 200 at a time while others stood nearby, watching the feast and waiting their turn. In Kansas City, Kan., the army staged a separate dinner for several hundred and also provided clothes for those who needed them.

By the turn of the century, these dinners were becoming spectacles. The biggest came in 1901 at Madison Square Garden in New York City. Twenty-five thousand people dined courtesy of contributions to the army, much of it raised in red kettles on New York street corners.

In Kansas City in 1905, the army fed 1,000 people at once at Convention Hall. At long tables, young and old and white and black sat down to dine on turkey, beef, cabbage, turnips, potatoes and more. Then came music from a Salvation Army band and a 500-voice chorus,

Feeding the poor

In Kansas City in 1905, the Salvation Army began Christmas Day by distributing 800 baskets of food at Convention Hall. Each basket was planned to contain enough food for five people, consisting of chicken, beef, potatoes, sugar, crackers, shredded wheat, bread, apples, oranges and pies. With baskets stacked more than 10 feet high, the doors of the hall were opened at 10 a.m.; by noon the baskets were gone. The qualification to receive a basket: Tell them you were hungry.

CHRISTMASTIME IN KANSAS CITY

1890-1918: A SEASON FOR CHARITY

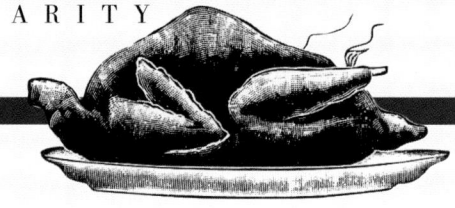

Christmas dinner ideas, 1890s

A week before Christmas 1897, *The Times* made these menu suggestions for the big day, beginning with "a fair sampling of a first-class dinner of the old colonial days":

Roast Turkey, Oyster Dressing.
Cranberry Sauce.
Mashed Potatoes.
Baked Corn.
Stewed Onions.
Chicken Pie.
Olives.   Pickled Peaches.
Pumpkin Pie.   Mince Pie.   Apple Pie.
Cheese.
Fruit.   Coffee.

Next came a menu "selected by a prominent French chef," combining plain fare with a few delicacies:

Raw Oysters,
Bullion.
Boiled Salmon.   Hollandaise Sauce.
Pickles, Boiled Potato Balls,
Salted Almonds.
Roast Turkey, Cranberry Sauce, Celery,
Mashed Potatoes, Scalloped Asparagus,
Chicken Pie.
Kirsch Punch.
Roast Duck, Currant Jelly,
Sweet Potato Croquettes.
Lettuce Salad, Sweetbreads.
Plum Pudding.   Brandy Sauce.
Mince Pie, Apple Pie, Cheese.
Ice Cream.   Cake.
Nuts, Raisins, Fruit.
Coffee.

Finally, the chef offered a third version:

Oysters on the Half-Shell.
Amber Soup.
Olives,   Salted Almonds,   Pickles.
Roast Turkey,   Giblet Sauce.
Cranberry Jelly, Celery, Cauliflower.
Mashed Potatoes,
Glazed Sweet Potatoes.
Pineapple Sherbet.
Broiled Quail, French Peas,
Currant Jelly.
Lettuce Salad.
Mince Pie,   Pumpkin Pie.
Ice Cream, Cake, Frozen Milk Punch.
Coffee,   Fruit.

and a stereopticon presentation with pictures from Bible stories, illustrations for the song, "Where Is My Wandering Boy Tonight?" and a portrait of President Theodore Roosevelt.

The event was not for the hungry only. In fact, the diners that Christmas night were outnumbered by several thousand spectators who paid admission and packed the boxes and balcony to watch the poor eat. They also chipped in for a collection taken during the program.

There would be plenty of opportunities for contributions. Charities, it seemed, were everywhere.

By 1915, the Provident Association, the Board of Public Welfare, the Good Fellows, the Minute Circle and the Women's City League had joined the Salvation Army and the efforts of the mayor's office in performing some kind of Christmas charitable service for the needy.

Inevitably, there were overlaps. Other problems were arising, too. Reports came back that some dinner-basket delivery trucks were rushed by neighborhood children in a state of near-riot. One truck's engine broke down, and a crowd of 200 gathered around it. Doubts arose about the worthiness of the recipients: Were all of them truly needy?

In 1916, City Hall was named a clearinghouse for several of these efforts. Investigators for the city's Board of Public Welfare and workers for the Health Department went over requests for food to try to verify the need. They prepared tickets that recipients had to sign to guard against duplication and theft, and to ensure that the right people received dinner baskets.

The work was done under the auspices of the Mayor's Christmas Tree Association. It signaled a new phase in an effort by the city's highest office, an effort that in 1916 was already decades old.

The mayors pitch in

In the late 1870s, Kansas City had become home to thousands of poor people. As a nexus of rail lines, the city collected people looking for work, and not all of them succeeded.

With no formal government organization to help the poor and with little organized charity at the time, the city's mayor, George M. Shelley, spent much of his time and energy on the problem. Lines of people formed at his office, looking for aid and employment and often getting it.

Christmastime, Shelley recalled decades later, was particularly hard on the suppliants. In 1878, using his own money, Shelley purchased baskets and groceries and prepared 1,000 dinners. On Christmas Eve he put up a tree. On Christmas Day the

VOLUNTEERS OF AMERICA FEEDING THE POOR OF THE SLUMS.

A dinner for the destitute

"The whole scene was very curious. There were pale-faced women with little babies, and the dullest imagination could not help but fancy all the dreariness of their lives. There were little dirty-faced boys and girls, and scores of men whose lives were apparently lived under a blight....Of course it must be understood there were many there of respectability and of worth. They simply were too poor to buy a dinner..."

— *Account in* The Times *of the Christmas dinner for the poor staged by the Volunteers of America on Dec. 24, 1899*

An artist captured these scenes from the 1908 Mayor's Christmas Tree children's party for *The Kansas City Times*.

food baskets were distributed to those who came to his City Hall office. The next year, the event was moved to a larger hall. Joined by colleagues and volunteers, the mayor played Santa Claus, entertaining and handing out food baskets to about 1,000 people.

Later mayors followed the tradition in different ways, as when Webster Smith in 1895 not only distributed baskets but also staged his banquet for newsboys and bootblacks.

In 1908, Mayor Thomas Crittenden and supporters did the traditional basket delivery and also raised $10,000 for a giant party for poor children in Convention Hall. Committees were formed and businesses called on for merchandise. A large tree stood on the platform surrounded by dinner baskets for poor families and candy and toys for the children.

That Christmas afternoon the sky was clear, temperatures were in the mid-40s and upwards of 7,000 children appeared at the hall at 13th and Central streets. That exceeded the number of presents available. Organizers hadn't counted on children coming from Kansas City,

The Good Fellows

A new kind of organized charity arose in Kansas City in the early 1900s, without mass gatherings, without spectacle and without individual public credit for the benefactors. The Good Fellows movement, invented in Chicago and publicized through *The Tribune*, arrived in Kansas City Dec. 17, 1909, by way of an article on the front page of *The Star*. A letter attributed to an unnamed "Grand Worthy Master of the National Lodge of Good Fellows" called on Kansas Citians with money to write the newspaper, telling their name, address and how many children they could help, and enclosing a stamp for return postage. From a list furnished by Kansas City charities, the Good Fellow applicant would receive by return mail from *The Star* the name, address, sex and age of the same number of needy children.

It was up to the Good Fellow to buy a gift of any value and deliver it directly to the recipient.

"You gain neither notoriety nor advertising," *The Star* wrote. "You deal with no organization; no record will be kept; your letter will be restored to you with its answer. The whole plan is as anonymous as old Santa Claus himself."

In the ensuing week, *The Star* published daily front-page articles encouraging potential Good Fellows to sign up.

By Christmas Eve, the newspaper announced that 1,000 children stood to receive presents from Good Fellows in Kansas City. A separate Good Fellow group in Independence planned to treat 200 more.

One particularly generous applicant distributed a carload of toys, candy and books around town, accompanied by a reporter. First he visited two ill children on the West Side, and then two more on Ninth Street, where the mother took in wash for a living. East of Brooklyn Avenue the benefactor left a package for a family of nine with no mother and a sick father.

Within five years Good Fellows were distributing more than 4,000 presents to the poor.

Oat bags

In 1909, the Kansas City chapter of the Humane Society sponsored its own food giveaway — free oat bags for the city's hungry horses. At Convention Hall on Christmas morning, horse owners who had received one of 500 cards distributed by the society could pick up 10-pound bags of oats. On each bag was written the animal's name; the owner also received printed instructions on how to care for a horse and a copy of *Black Beauty*. Also available were horse blankets.

Savings clubs

In support of the gift-giving splurge, banks instituted Christmas Clubs. The first one appeared in 1910. Its members saved money throughout the year for spending at Christmas.

1890-1918: A SEASON FOR CHARITY

Kan.

Thirty policemen organized them into lines of boys and girls, some of whom were accompanied by parents. Portable gangways kept them in manageable lines and each child's hand was stamped with a tree logo to prevent repeat customers. Each received a sack containing five toys, a game, an orange, a banana, an apple, a box of candy and nuts.

For the thousand or so who didn't get presents, a second event was scheduled for the next afternoon. Organizers that day decided to make such an event annual by chartering the Mayor's Christmas Tree Association.

Heady times, then wartime

For Kansas Citians who did have money, the new century brought hundreds of new opportunities to spend it. Christmastime became the most important season of the year for retailers, here and everywhere. Competition was booming, and by the mid-1910s Christmas advertisements were appearing well before Thanksgiving.

Toy Oldsmobile of 1905.

Curbside merchants

An annual event Downtown was the appearance of sidewalk merchants peddling turn-of-the-century action toys. At Ninth and Walnut streets in 1905 one peddler, using a concealed string, manipulated two small figures that alternately boxed and danced with each other.

"Make the little ones at home laugh by the hour on Christmas morning," he told passersby.

A block west on Main Street, a sidewalk merchant sold colorful spinning tops at 25 cents each. Across the street, a woman sold windup toy automobiles. Up Main Street, a man sold bird whistles, tin model cars, holly wreaths and mistletoe sprays.

One peddler confided to a reporter that he came from New York with his stock of toys and would head home as soon as he was sold out. "Just put it in your notebook," he told the reporter, "that I manage to eat all right."

Sent from Kansas City to Pleasant Hill in Cass County in 1915.

Christmas cards

In the 1890s, the Christmas card field was taken over by German card manufacturers, who printed colorful Christmas images on the front of postcards. These two-sided cards lasted until American card manufacturers such as Hall Brothers of Kansas City and Gibson arose in the 1910s. Their cards typically were folded, with an illustration and message on the cover, a longer message within. The National Association of Greeting Card Manufacturers was formed in 1913. The organization conducted advertising campaigns encouraging use of the cards, and advised retailers when and how best to display them. The industry prospered, and German dominance receded.

Santa's message was clearly commercial in a 1911 card mailed by the Jones Dry Goods Co., top left. The rest were personal cards sent from the Kansas City area in the 1910s.

CHRISTMASTIME IN KANSAS CITY

1890-1918: A SEASON FOR CHARITY

Just a fad

As the shopping season ended in 1907, New York toy dealers were reporting the end of the latest craze — the Teddy bear. In 1906, stores couldn't get enough of the bears and so laid in a big supply for 1907, but were unable to clear their shelves. Other stuffed animals, however, sold well, among them dogs, elephants, monkeys and rabbits.

Yes, Virginia...

In December 1897, the place of Santa Claus in popular myth was cemented by Francis Church, editor of the *New York Sun*. In a brief article that was to become famous, Church replied to a letter from 8-year-old Virginia O'Hanlon, asking, "Is there a Santa Claus?"

"Yes, Virginia," Church wrote, "there is a Santa Claus." No one can see him, he continued, yet "the most real things in the world are those that neither children nor men can see." He suggested that Santa existed partly because people *must* believe in such a figure. Santa would endure, he said, "to make glad the heart of childhood."

An Independence child's letter to Santa Claus, 1898.

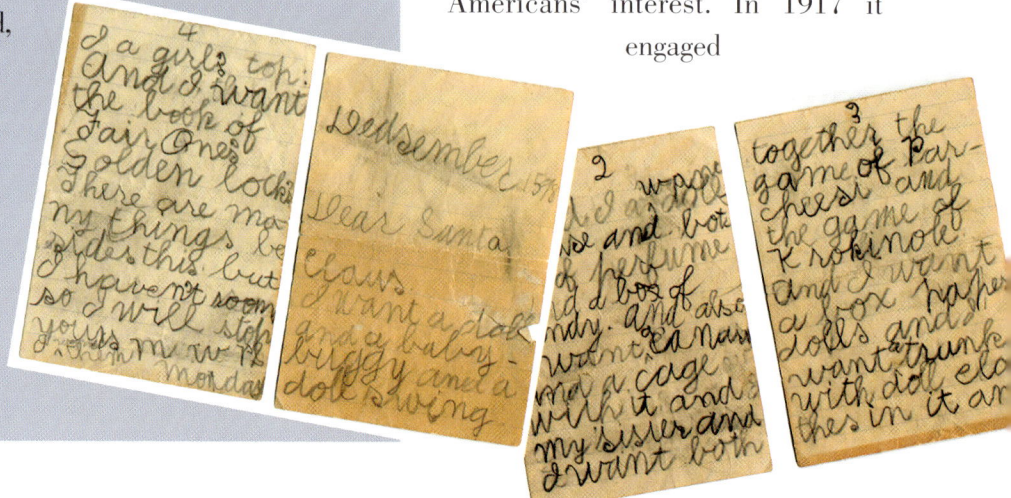

On Nov. 17, 1916, Bunting Hardware promoted its "Grand Toy Opening" and promised "Santa Claus will be in our store Saturday." There was plenty of shopping time that day; Bunting stayed open until 9 p.m. A few days later, Gillette offered its shaving sets as "Happiness for *His* Christmas Day." And on Nov. 24, the John Taylor Dry Goods Co. on Main Street at Petticoat Lane advertised "Christmas suggestions" — dolls, tags and seals, petticoats, fancy aprons and ribbons — under a drawing of a wreath.

These were the stirrings of the all-out consumer Christmas we know today. Before it reached full flower, however, the country made a jolting change of course.

Since 1914, the war among the powers of Europe had engaged Americans' interest. In 1917 it engaged

Americans themselves. The United States officially entered the European conflict that April, and American troops were landing in France by June. By October, they were in the trenches.

Suddenly, life at home was different. The government began urging families to conserve resources considered important for the war effort. "Wheatless Mondays and Wednesdays," "meatless Tuesdays" and "porkless Thursdays and Saturdays" were promoted. Sugar was rationed and what sugar was available was expensive.

Holiday cooking had to change, and along with it holiday shopping.

The 1917 Christmas rush began earlier than ever, spurred by shoppers hoping to deliver presents in time for Christmas to soldiers in France or at forts and bases in the United States. The government also encouraged early shopping on the theory that salesmen and deliverymen could finish their work well before the holiday, and then become available for the armed services.

Emery, Bird, Thayer Co. and the Jones Dry Goods Co. advertised on the weekend before Thanksgiving that only 24 shopping days remained

At Christmastime 1915, this shop at Union Station offered an array of toys.

Capital of the midlands

By Christmas season 1909, Kansas City merchants were beginning to notice more patrons coming to town from farther away. Some railroads ran excursion trains from central Iowa, and from western Illinois, meaning Kansas City was competing with cities like Chicago, St. Louis and Springfield. It was already a given that the city's trade territory stretched far to the Southwest, including Oklahoma, Texas and New Mexico.

Said the manager of Emery, Bird, Thayer: "We find that we are invading more and more the territory other cities claim."

By this time, Kansas City, Mo., alone boasted almost a quarter-million people and was the 20th-largest city in the United States. Kansas City, Kan., had almost 100,000 people.

Holiday fatigue

A rapidly moving world and the rise in the need to purchase gifts helped spur early public utterances of Christmas burn-out.

"Somehow or other Christmas ... doesn't allow you any rest, what with one thing and another," one man wrote a friend in 1889.

In 1894 the *New York Tribune* declared that the "modern expansion of the custom of giving Christmas presents has done more than anything else to rob Christmas of its traditional joyousness ... As soon as the Thanksgiving turkey is eaten, the great question of buying Christmas presents begins to take the terrifying shape it has come to assume in recent years."

The same was happening in Kansas City, as *The Star* acknowledged in 1907. Even while defending the worthiness of Christmas and its hoopla, the newspaper laid out a case that the season was becoming a trial:

"It is not to be denied that Christmas makes a lot of work and causes plenty of botheration. It never comes and goes that you don't hear folks who are normally amiable ... speak of it as a nuisance and express the wish that it might never come again. The cost of Christmas to very many persons is quite an item; but the vexation incident to the selection of gifts and their adaptation to the persons for whom they are designed is even more serious than the expense.

A cartoonist's view of the holiday hustle and bustle, from *The Star*, Dec. 17, 1905.

"So, aside from the children, whose especial institution Christmas is ... the passing of the day is hailed with a sense of relief and gladness ....

"But what is there in life worth having that doesn't involve labor and create worry? Children are a constant source of trouble, but what would the world be without them? Homemaking is attended by trials and difficulties, but what are these as compared with the barren existence which is endured by people who live in boarding houses and hotels?

"By wiping out Christmas you would eliminate, let us concede, days and weeks of the stew and the fever and the fuss which always comes with it; but where, after all, would we find compensation for the keen and eager excitement which it spreads abroad?

"Let it be admitted that we make more bother out of Christmas than is necessary; but it would be better to fuss more about it even than we do than to do without it altogether."

— *Editorial,* The Star, *Dec. 25, 1907*

Christmas in a small apartment: Immigrants from Germany, the Mauersberger family sat for its Christmas Day photograph in 1913 in their combination bedroom and sitting room at 314 W. 17th St.

until Christmas. Merchants reported an unprecedented rush.

Then came a few weeks' lull, yet the streets and stores were jammed again by mid-December. Those shoppers heard something new in 1917 — people stationed at intersections, loudly promoting the membership drive of the American Red Cross. The campaign proved successful, and it was topped off by a Christmas Eve carol sing in cities across America.

In Kansas City, seven hundred groups of children sang carols at homes displaying the Red Cross emblem that night. When the caroling began, the temperature was 22 degrees and a strong wind made things uncomfortable. As the carolers

Christmas memories

"The Barzens across the street had a huge Christmas tree. They were of German extraction and they canvassed their drawing room floor (for it). We just had a smaller Christmas tree in our upstairs living room.

"I remember getting a doll. That was the one time that I found there was no Santa Claus. I'd seen in Mother's chest in her room — I'd seen a little yellow knitted set for a doll. That was under our Christmas tree. I was beginning to suspect, anyway."

— *Dorothy D. Stanley (born in 1892) on her childhood in Kansas City.*

"I don't know how Mother ever did it, but she always had a very nice (Christmas) meal. We never had turkey; that was very unusual. Turkeys were not raised in big quantities and shipped in cold storage like they are today, frozen. You had to get them fresh. They were very expensive. You could go to City Market and get them, but you had to kill them and bring them home yourself."

—*Doris K. Gorman (born 1901).*

She and Dorothy Stanley were interviewed in 1985 for an oral history project.

1890-1918: A SEASON FOR CHARITY

A community tree

In 1915, Kansas City's first community Christmas tree was installed on the plaza in front of Union Station by the Women's City League. The next year, Kansas City, Kan., had its own community tree in Huron Square. The two Kansas Citys joined Cleveland, Pittsburgh, Baltimore and almost 100 other cities across the United States staging similar civic celebrations.

On Christmas Eve 1917, *The Star* offered this wartime sentiment.

trooped from house to house, block to block, some homeowners came out to welcome the groups of children. Some invited them inside to get warm.

"This Christmas Eve is one which Kansas City long should remember," Henry D. Ashley, chairman of the Red Cross Christmas carols committee, told a reporter for *The Star*. "We may as well announce now that this is to be an annual event until the war is over."

Yet before Christmas could come around again, the war was over. For months after the November 1918 armistice, various wartime restrictions remained in force. Many troops did not return from France until spring 1919.

Once they did, life in the United States would change markedly. The country entered the modern era of radio, blockbuster movies, ubiquitous advertising, inexpensive automobiles and a booming stock market.

The trappings of Christmas kept pace.

On Christmas Eve 1918, with transportation brought to its knees, Kansas Citians fought through the snow. An artist for *The Star* offered this view and the one on the following page under the title, "Eleven inches of snow!"

White Christmas in Kansas City? Once in a while…

A snow-covered Christmas — although commonly wished for, sung about, and used as a seasonal symbol — is not the norm in Kansas City. At least since the government began keeping weather statistics in 1889, relatively few Christmases have seen snow on the ground, let alone falling. But when the snow did arrive, it was occasionally a doozy.

The snowiest Christmas on record occurred in 1918, the year the first World War ended. On Dec. 23, with streetcar operators on strike and the Christmas shopping season at its peak, a snowstorm struck. Three inches fell that day, and the temperature stayed below freezing.

Downtown was jammed, and cab companies could not meet demand. Drivers of jitneys, which were automobiles or vans that transported people along certain routes, either abandoned their vehicles altogether or raised fares exorbitantly. Some automobile owners offered rides, but also asked high prices. Late workers and theatergoers tried to get rooms in hotels. A messenger boy reported that it had taken three hours to cross the Intercity Viaduct into Missouri and return to the Kansas side. Pedestrians were found wandering in the heavy snow, dazed and lost.

A policeman told this unhappy tale of trying to handle long lines of slow-moving automobiles:

"We do not have a chance in the world. I am about frozen, and a minute ago I started waving my arms to restore circulation and the drivers thought I was giving signals, and the first thing I knew there were cars coming down on me from four different directions. It took me 15 minutes to get them straightened

1890-1918: A SEASON FOR CHARITY

out."

The snowfall did not taper off until the morning of Christmas Eve. It totaled 11 inches. The temperature dropped that evening and remained under 20 degrees on Christmas Day.

Trains coming to Kansas City from the south and west were delayed, most by hours, and many passengers spent the night at Union Station. Yet Christmas Eve had its pleasures. A War Camp Community sing scheduled at the station came off as planned, and the crowd was swelled to about 3,000 by stranded soldiers, sailors and civilians. Outside, the community Christmas tree sparkled amid the snow with red, white and blue lights — in honor of the recently completed war.

And on Christmas Day, Kansas City's government weather observer, Patrick Connor, called the weather ideal.

"A cloudless sky, with a temperature not severe yet low enough to prevent thaw and consequent slush," he said, "were nature's contributions to the perfect day."

The 1910s were the area's best decade for white Christmases. A little more than an inch lay on the ground on Christmas Day 1913, 6 in 1914 and 4 in 1915.

Before the beginning of official weather record-keeping, snows were recalled that were of legendary dimensions. On Oct. 29, 1829, Clay County was covered by 20 inches of snow, which was augmented a week later with a similar amount, leaving a ground cover of 2 feet. On Jan. 3, 1830, more snow fell. That storm, reported in *A History of Clay and Platte Counties* more than three decades later, added to what was on the ground and created a cover of 3 feet. Evidently, Christmas 1829 just past had been exceedingly white.

By mid-century, newspaper reports described white Christmases in glowing terms. In its Christmas-Day issue of 1860, the *Journal of Commerce* said:

"On Thursday night the snow commenced falling, on Friday and Saturday it was continued at intervals, on Sunday night, a still heavier fall increased its depth, and yesterday it continued to fall without intermission for the greater part of the day, until now we have the best sleighing snow that has been witnessed here for four or five years past. A sleighing snow at Christmas times makes a Christmas worth having."

Nine years later, *The Times* described a sleighing party that traveled to Westport for a concert, and returned "under the stars as merry and joyous as the young always are on winter nights to the music of the sleighbells."

About 2 inches fell early Christmas Day 1895, according to *The Star*, and "when the dawn came the snow lay in a

> A sleighing snow at Christmas times makes a Christmas worth having."
>
> — Journal of Commerce, *1860*

blanket of pure white on streets and housetops and fields....It lasted long enough for sleigh rides...."

Measurable snowfall on Christmas Day occurred in 1892, 1895, 1899 and 1900. In the 20th century, it occurred on Christmas Day itself only seven times. The latest was in 1987, when three-tenths of an inch was measured. The deepest was in 1962, which amounted to 1.3 inches (adding to 3 inches already on the ground), and the next deepest was the half-inch that fell Christmas Day two years later.

Other Christmases have been white because of earlier snow and temperatures cold enough to preserve it. Even so, only 16 times in the 20th century would Kansas City awaken to a Christmas morning with more than an inch of snow on the ground. In the snowiest December on record, 1961, snow drifted as much as 6 feet deep in parts of rural Jackson County, marooning some families. Eight inches were reported on level ground as of Christmas morning.

On Christmas 1924, 7 inches was measured on the ground.

Some other notable snow-covered Christmases occurred at mid-century: 4.2 inches in 1945, 5 inches in 1948, one inch in 1949, 2 inches in 1952 and 5 inches in 1953.

Among late-century Christmases with memorable snow already on the ground was the deep-freeze season of 1983, when high temperatures the week before the holiday never exceeded single digits and preserved 7 inches of snow. Four inches were on the ground Christmas Day 1989, preserved by a few days of below-zero cold. And in 1997, 3 inches were on the ground on Christmas Day.

Having fun with the weatherman: For decades Patrick Connor was Kansas City's weather forecaster. In 1915, he missed a prediction and received this Christmas Eve lampooning from *The Star*.

5 | 1919-1945
Dressed in holiday style

"Everything at your fingertips:" This catalog for the Country Club Plaza boasted about its growing number of stores.

U.S. industry had geared up production for the war effort. With the arrival of peace, it could turn out a host of new products in vast quantities. Right away, retailers figured out how to get Americans to buy them.

In print, on billboards, on radio, on the streets and sidewalks, advertising and promotion were appearing as never before. Increasingly merchants were using several avenues at once — including public festivals, occasions and displays — to move their wares. As the biggest retailing season of the year, Christmas would see the grandest of these efforts.

Consider this multimedia marketing campaign staged in 1929 in Kansas City:

On Monday, Nov. 18, readers were alerted by their morning newspaper that radio engineers at WDAF had received some mysterious signals the night before — signals coming from above the Arctic Circle! "Rap-tap-tap-rap-tap-tap," went the sounds, according to the newspaper account, which said the engineers expected the same thing every 24 hours. Tune in to WDAF that night at 6:15, the advice went; children might be best able to tell what the sounds were.

On Tuesday evening, children could hear the "rap-tap" sounds themselves, only this time they ended with a "ping." Slowly, the story unfolded.

On Wednesday, a miniature fairy named Crystal was described on the broadcast and also in the next morning's newspaper; she had ridden her miniature reindeer, Snowflake, around the WDAF microphone. Thursday brought nursery-rhyme characters to the broadcast. It also brought mail from children guessing at the mystery of the "rap-tap." From south Kansas City, from Lenexa, Nortonville, Highland and LaCygne, Kan., from Cowgill, Mo., the letters came. Most of them guessed that it was a message from Santa Claus. At least one writer tossed in her Christmas gift wish. As the weekend arrived, a voice could be heard, laughing. By Monday evening, it was identified as that of

Beginning in the 1920s, downtown was decked out in greenery and oversized ornaments in an effort to create a unified Christmas look. This was the 1100 block of Grand Avenue in the early 1930s.

1919-1945: DRESSED IN HOLIDAY STYLE

By the late 1920s, Christmas tree lights appeared in a variety of decorative designs.

Santa Claus.

Tuesday night came the payoff announcement: Santa was coming to Kansas City! He would ride in a big parade downtown on Saturday morning, start of the first big shopping weekend of the holiday season.

That's how *The Kansas City Star* used its radio station, WDAF, and its morning edition, *The Times*, to promote the event. The idea was to bring good will (and probably advertising) to the newspaper, and business to the merchants — all by drawing people downtown.

The growing metropolis provided a rich potential market. The two Kansas Citys were on their way to topping 540,000 by 1930, a 21 percent increase in their combined population in a single decade.

This new age began in 1919. Once wartime restrictions were lifted, financial markets turned bullish across the United States. In Kansas City that year, Christmas shoppers mobbed downtown. On Saturday, Dec. 21, with four shopping days left until Christmas (on Sundays stores were closed) shoppers clogged the sidewalks all day. Clerks couldn't keep up, and when the shopping was

Union Station sing

From 1925 to 1937, a Christmas sing was an annual event in the Grand Hall of Union Station. The performances were begun by Mabelle Glenn, music supervisor of the Kansas City School District. High school choirs sang from the balconies, and a band played from the floor. On at least one carol each year, hundreds of travelers joined in.

The 1930 sing came on Christmas Eve, just before the ceremonial lighting of the Mayor's Christmas tree outside. A thousand high school singers from Westport, Lincoln, Paseo, Southwest, Northeast, Manual, East and Central performed, one school at a time. A choral director and master of ceremonies who stood atop the ticket booth led all the choirs and the travelers in "Adeste Fidelis," O, Little Town of Bethlehem" and "Silent Night."

In 1938, the carol sing was moved to Municipal Auditorium to provide more room for the audience and clearer acoustics than the marble-floored Grand Hall.

"At Christmas time...Blanche Morrison's chorus from Lincoln High School would go to the Union Station and get up in the balcony .... We'd sing Christmas carols as visitors and tourists came in from the trains. That would be the last day of school before the Christmas vacation. That would be quite an occasion."

— *Helen Gertrude Bardwell of Kansas City, interviewed for a 1985 oral history project.*

1919-1945: DRESSED IN HOLIDAY STYLE

done, streetcars and jitneys couldn't move them out fast enough. The post office opened on Sunday to keep packages moving; the postmaster reported an increase of more than 50 percent in the mails since the Christmas before.

The rest of the days up to Christmas 1919 were equally frantic. Aisles of department stores were packed shoulder to shoulder as late as Christmas Eve. Shoppers arrived from all over the region. For the first time since Union Station opened in 1914, all 20 ticket windows were busy on Dec. 24, and each had a line most of the day.

In Kansas City, like cities around the country, Christmas was going public.

A sight for everyone

The process had begun in a small way before World War I, when Kansas City and others mounted community trees and held community music programs.

In the 1920s the idea was captured by merchants. In addition to making their own window displays increasingly impressive, merchants banded together to create displays that changed the appearance of entire

From the modest Shell gasoline station at 85th Street and Holmes Road to the massive Jones Store Co. at 12th and Main streets, merchants dressed their stores in holiday finery in the mid-1930s.

68   CHRISTMASTIME IN KANSAS CITY

December 1929 found merchants near 31st Street and Troost Avenue installing their own common displays. Below: A light snow dusted the decorations in the 1000 block of Walnut Street in December 1936.

shopping districts.

In 1924, Kansas City's downtown retailers joined to sponsor displays of greenery, which wrapped utility poles and hung from power lines along major streets. In 1929, a corridor of greenery — heavy spruce garlands — went up along Main and Walnut streets and Grand Avenue. Wrapped with it was a carload of vines imported from the South. More than 6,000 electrical connections were necessary for lighting. Along Petticoat Lane, stars hung from the

1919-1945: DRESSED IN HOLIDAY STYLE

The Country Club Plaza

garlands. Spruce trees topped trolley-wire poles and garlands reached across sidewalks. Bows made of cardboard covered with glitter added daytime color.

Out south a new shopping district, the Country Club Plaza, sprang up in the 1920s, the brainchild of developer J.C. Nichols. Beginning with a small string of lights in 1925 and expanding rapidly each year, the Plaza by 1928 was being called a "nighttime fairyland." Across Brush Creek, the nine-story Villa Serena apartment hotel boasted 1,200 bulbs in five colors. With these decorations came motorists, their cars idling, staring at the Plaza display and its nearby accompaniments.

The idea was spreading across town. Along Troost Avenue from 31st Street, yet another business district had garlands and stars hanging above streets and sidewalks.

America's first big commercial Christmas parade was staged by Gimbel's Department store in New York in 1920. The event was set for Thanksgiving, aiming to give a ceremonial early start to the Christmas shopping season. Four years later, Hudson's in Detroit sponsored a parade there. The same

In 1928 the budding shopping district attached greenery to light standards along 47th Street, above, for day-and-night holiday decoration. Parents could take their children in the mid-1930s to visit Santa Claus at his "headquarters" at Ward Parkway and Broadway.

When the lights came on, the Plaza shone, above in December 1936. A shorter-lived decoration was this giant Santa. The early color photograph was taken in December 1932.

CHRISTMASTIME IN KANSAS CITY

1919-1945: DRESSED IN HOLIDAY STYLE

year, Macy's weighed in with its parade in New York; it ended with the triumphal appearance of Santa Claus.

Soon Kansas City had versions of these. In 1925, a Santa Claus character was escorted by a police marching band in a quick noon-hour parade through downtown. It occurred at midweek, barring all but the youngest children from attending because school was still in session.

That problem was fixed in the grandiose parade of 1929, scheduled for the Saturday after Thanksgiving, when school was out. Children were clearly the objective; the elaborate "teaser" campaign on radio and in the newspaper was aimed right at them.

At 10 a.m. that Saturday, in the middle of what was becoming one of the biggest shopping weekends of the holiday season, a parade of floats depicting children's stories headed down Grand Avenue. In the lead was Old King Cole on horseback, followed by the Ararat Shrine Band. Then came a float depicting a cow jumping over the moon, then the Westport High School marching band, and so on. The sidewalks were jammed a dozen people deep with children standing in front or sitting on the shoulders of adults. Overhead,

Floats and spectators lined Grand Avenue for the Santa Claus parade in late November 1929.

Straight from his headquarters in "Icy Cape" and equipped with a microphone and loudspeaker, Santa Claus delighted children from the final float in the parade. "Ho! Ho! Ho!" he called out. "I know that little girl! I know you all!" Below right: Spewing its own cloud, a miniature train was part of the procession.

CHRISTMASTIME IN KANSAS CITY

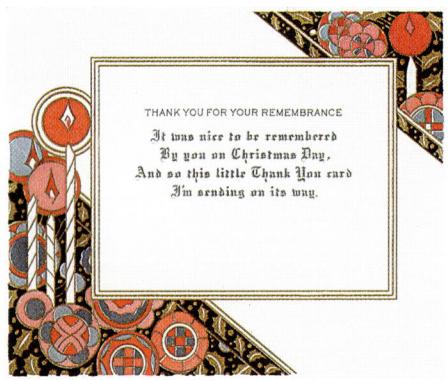
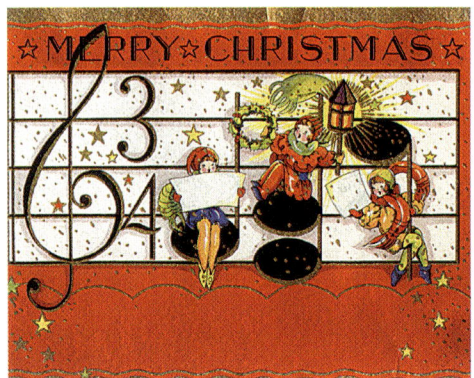

Christmas cards from the 1920s.

Kansas City's skyscraper City Hall, completed in 1937, was dressed up each evening with lighted stars on its lower floors. Office lights on the upper floors were left on in the form of a cross.

Emery, Bird, Thayer trotted out a few of the finer things for men and women in its 1934 Christmas catalog. The department store, one of Kansas City's oldest, offered a set of golf clubs for $43.50 and a full-length fur coat for $195.

garlands, wreaths and stars framed the scene. The final float carried Santa, his sleigh and reindeer.

The next day, *The Star* published letters of thanks from the school board presidents of the two Kansas Citys.

"Santa Claus and his imposing spectacle of Mother Goose characters that visited Kansas City yesterday not only gladdened the hearts of thousands of children, but also established a new spirit of Christmas by the family firesides," wrote John E. Carlson of the Kansas City, Kan., board.

Yet even as one more free-spending Christmas was passing, the country's financial markets were signaling that an end was about to come.

1919-1945: DRESSED IN HOLIDAY STYLE

Toy Town got a big push in the Emery, Bird, Thayer promotional effort. This book of illustrations was accompanied by a poem made to order for the store.

The Santa Claus we love so well
Away up north is known to dwell.
Kris makes the toys and dollies too
Which Emery, Bird, Thayer's bring to you.

Kris, well wrapped from head to feet,
Jumps in his sleigh and takes his seat.
Then quickly all the reindeer start;
To Emery, Bird, Thayer's next they dart.

Emery, Bird, Thayer's big Toy Town
Enjoys well-merited renown.
And children help old Kris to choose
By telling Santa Claus their views!

While youngsters sleep, dolls aeroplane—
But falling, never feel a pain.
Around Toy Town the dollies fly—
In Emery, Bird, Thayer's mounting high.

Emery, Bird, Thayer's Toy Town elves
Are ready to enjoy themselves.
So children's games the dollies seek,
But play in ways that are unique.

Some dollies act they are a mother—
Just as girls do with one another.
Emery, Bird, Thayer's tots are fed;
The smallest dolls must go to bed!

Santa's number, you should know,
Is Harrison, three-five-one-oh.
Emery, Bird, Thayer's telephone
To dolls and children is well known!

Because the dolls can sit outside,
They like an Emery, Bird, Thayer ride.
A ticket is not used for fare,
But yet the train goes everywhere.

To see the toys that always please,
Be sure to visit E.-B.-T.'s!
"E.-B.-T.," to girls and boys,
Of course means "Every Body's Toys!"

On Christmas eve Kris does his part;
From Emery, Bird, Thayer's playthings start.
When children are in bed asleep,
Then down the chimney he will creep.

E is for Emery—Emery, Bird, Thayer;
M stands for Merry—toys make your home gayer.
E is for Everything with which to play;
R stands for Reindeer, which pull Santa's sleigh;
Y is for Youngsters, who love toys each day.

B stands for Bird and Babies as well;
I is for Infants whose playthings they sell.
R is a letter that well means Reliable;
D means Dependable—all goods are buyable.

T stands for Thayer and likewise for Toys;
H is the Happiness each child enjoys.
A means Assortments in toys of all kinds;
Y is for You—warm welcomes one finds.
E stands for Enter, Toy Town is here;
R is Re-enter all through the year!

Emery, Bird, Thayer Company
TOY TOWN   FIFTH FLOOR

CHRISTMASTIME IN KANSAS CITY

1919-1945: DRESSED IN HOLIDAY STYLE

In the stores and all around

Hall's on 11th Street was stocked with its cards, of which some 1930s examples are below. Right: Children posed for a photo on a reindeer figure at the Jones Store Co. downtown in 1927.

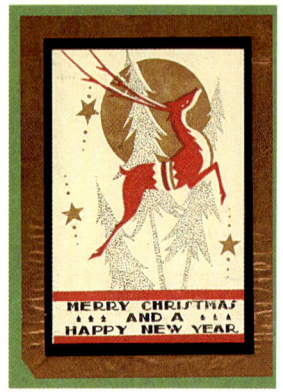

Streetcar Santa

At Christmastime, streetcars, buses and trolley buses were promoted as a useful means of avoiding parking problems. Below: The motorman on this specially decorated streetcar wore a Santa Claus outfit.

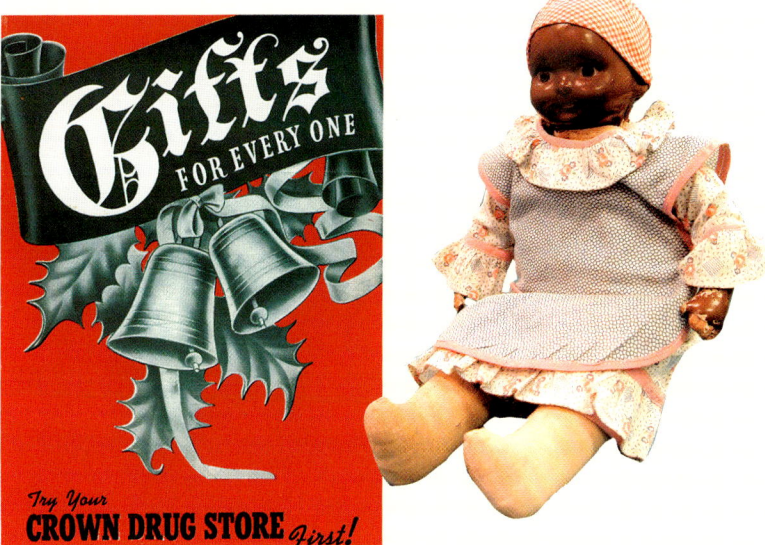

Above, left to right: The lower facade of Kline's department store on Walnut Street was a mass of greenery in 1928. The Crown Drug Co., founded in Kansas City, had scores of stores in three states by the 1930s. This doll was produced about 1920.

CHRISTMASTIME IN KANSAS CITY

1919-1945: DRESSED IN HOLIDAY STYLE

"The Good Old Days" were not quite two years in the past when S.J. Ray drew this editorial cartoon for *The Star* of Dec. 20, 1931.

Slowing down

On Wall Street in late October 1929, stocks had taken a serious fall. Already, automobile sales, manufacturing output and construction were declining nationwide. By autumn 1930, a wave of business liquidations spread across the country. In 1930, consumer spending fell 10 percent, a clear blow to the commercial aspect of Christmastime and to all the retailers who depended on it for a profit.

In Kansas City, an early December weekend told the story of falling prices. At John Taylor Dry Goods Co., men's ties that were advertised for $1 on the first December weekend in 1929 were priced at 55 cents a year later. Women's underwear called dancettes cost $3.95 in 1929, $1.95 in 1930.

At the Jones Store bargain basement, silk hosiery dropped from 95 cents to 75 cents and winter coats from $16.75 to $14.95. Cloche hats advertised from $1.69 to $3.69 in 1929 were all advertised for $1.29 in 1930.

The sidewalks were crowded with browsers and shoppers in early December 1930. Yet even if they had

Free Christmas dinners brought big Depression-era crowds to the City Union Mission, above, and to Thomas J. Pendergast's annual feed. The Pendergast crowd at Sixth and Main streets in 1932, left, numbered more than 4,000. It was the largest to that time.

1919-1945: DRESSED IN HOLIDAY STYLE

bought as much as the year before, merchants clearly were not going to make as much money.

Within three years, the Depression would throw more than a quarter of all Americans out of work. Within four years, the gross national product would be half what it was in 1929. Credit dried up, throwing a damper over the entire retail economy, led by the Christmas season.

Retail merchants struggled. In mid-December 1931 many employers, encouraged by the Merchants Association, gave workers a half-day off for shopping before Christmas. The merchants hoped the extra time would stimulate their business. The same year, most justice-of-the-peace courts in Jackson County declared a two-week moratorium on garnishments of paychecks from mid-December until after Christmas.

Christmas charities for the poor also showed the stark difference. In the late 1920s the Mayor's Christmas Tree Association was distributing about 4,500 dinner baskets each Christmas. In 1930, that number jumped to 7,000. Within three years the Christmas-basket program, which

A rousing good time: The Mayor's Christmas Tree party for youngsters on Dec. 26, 1932, in Convention Hall.

The mayor's party — a child's-eye view

When he was 8 or 9 years old, in the mid-1920s, Frank Pisciotta's older sister took him and other siblings to the Mayor's Christmas Tree at Convention Hall. Here's how Pisciotta recalled the occasion in a 1985 interview for an oral history project of the Kansas City Museum.

"They would give everybody ... a stocking full of candy and a toy. I got one of those metal drums. I liked that drum so well that I kept that for three years. It lasted me three years.

"They used to try to take us every Christmas. That was a lot of fun. We used to see Santa Claus and they used to give a little play and things like that, you know.

"We got there by streetcar. That was our transportation in those days. We never had a car in the family."

The big tree

In 1916 the Mayor's Christmas Tree Association became the umbrella for several charitable groups' holiday food distribution. Its organizers decided to sponsor the community tree.

For several decades afterward, the large tree designated as the Mayor's Christmas Tree stood near Union Station, sometimes in the plaza in front, sometimes in Washington Square across the street.

On Christmas Eve 1925 Mayor Albert Beach hit the switch that turned on the lights while a streetcar employees' band played "Jingle Bells." Over the next few years, the Mayor's Christmas Tree Association set up trees in various parts of the city. In 1927, 12 trees with colored electric lights, cornucopias and candy canes were placed at such sites as 18th Street and the Paseo, Garrison Square, Budd Park, Mulkey Square, and Westport Road and Broadway. That plan was scrubbed by the 1930s because of vandalism.

The 1930 tree was in reality a collection of evergreens. It comprised a steel tower mounted on a concrete base. Three hundred small trees were attached to the tower and 500 lights strung on them.

Mayor Albert Beach and colleagues at the Mayor's tree near Union Station in the late 1920s.

CHRISTMASTIME IN KANSAS CITY

1919-1945: DRESSED IN HOLIDAY STYLE

Children were the special guests at a pageant staged by the Donnelly Garment Co. at the Pla-Mor Ballroom on Main Street in December 1939.

Even when the real things were still in service, model steam railroad locomotives were popular for kids — and many parents. This is a Lionel model made about 1940.

depended on a tag day for contributions, did not have enough money to continue despite continuing demand for the baskets.

The political machine of Thomas J. Pendergast each year served free Christmas dinner on the North Side to anyone who appeared. In the 1920s, this numbered about 2,000. In 1930, the dinner served 3,000. By the mid-1930s, 5,000 were partaking and the number almost reached 8,000 in 1938. The City Union Mission and Helping Hand Institute were serving at least 2,000 each year.

Struggling to soften the effects of the downturn, Kansas City and Jackson County voters in 1931 approved a 10-year plan of public works. From it would rise a new City Hall, a new Jackson County Courthouse, Municipal Auditorium, improvements at the airport and miles of new roads. This meant jobs and helped support consumer spending.

Despite that, by the mid-1930s one in 10 Kansas Citians was on relief. And although this was half the rate of many similar cities, the local economy was foundering. Outside the 10-year plan, construction activity

The wide-open town

Prohibition arrived officially on New Year's Day 1920, but the clamps were put on earlier in 1919, when Congress extended wartime prohibition until the 18th Amendment went into effect.

That's why one man at 12th Street and Baltimore Avenue, spotting several drunks among the crowd of shoppers on the last weekend before Christmas 1919 asked, "Where do they get it?"

Yet it was small wonder that you could "get it" at a lot of places in Kansas City, which had a notorious history of easy-flowing drink. For decades liquor laws and their enforcement had depended on the party and faction in power, and also upon whom liquor merchants sided with.

Four days before Christmas 1925, police, sheriff's and prosecutor's deputies spent from 6 p.m. to midnight raiding 58 places for illegal liquor. They recovered about 20,000 bottles of home brew, dragged in a dozen stills and seized or destroyed almost 1,000 gallons of liquor. One hundred thirty-eight sellers and buyers were jailed.

Even efforts like that were to no avail in a wide-open town where rackets flourished under the rule of the Pendergast political machine.

In December 1928 a group of prominent men complained to the federal and state governments that liquor sales were thriving and contributing to crime. Pointing to "dives existing here under the guise of soft drink parlors," they said such conditions could not exist "unless some sort of protection flourished....It is ridiculous to say that conditions could be as bad as they are without officials knowing what was going on and winking at it."

Their complaint was made two days after a Kansas City woman wielding an ax routed the clientele of a saloon her husband frequented. She was angered because her husband had spent $60 buying liquor "down by the Union Station," where he found "liquor flowing all around."

At Christmas 1929, forty-eight people found a way to get drunk enough for police to notice. They were taken to headquarters on charges of "too much cheer," but were freed as soon as they were able to recall where they lived.

Prohibition was revoked in early December 1933, but state and local law still prohibited taverns from staying open past midnight — or it was supposed to.

In 1937, *The Star* reported that police were cracking down on nightspot operators who let their Saturday night patrons keep drinking into Sunday. Henceforth, the word went out, owners had to remove patrons by dawn Sunday — which was a mere six hours later than the law required.

The fall of the Pendergast machine after the boss's imprisonment in 1939 and the ascension of reformist politicians tightened enforcement.

From *The Star*, Dec. 22, 1934.

1919-1945: DRESSED IN HOLIDAY STYLE

The Fairy Princess

"My very favorite thing was at Kline's department store. They had the Christmas fairy. She was better than Santa Claus, I thought, because you would tell her what you wanted for Christmas and then she would wave her magic wand and hit against this chute, and a package would fly down. You always got a little gift. That was 10 times better than Santa because you got nothing from Santa but promises."

— *Barbara Gorman (born in 1940), on growing up in Kansas City. Interviewed in 1985 for a Kansas City Museum oral history project.*

Kline's department store had its own twist on Christmas legend, introducing a Fairy Princess in 1935 when the store expanded and opened a Toyland. The Fairy Princess was its ruler. Parents bought tickets for children to speak to her. For each child, she waved a wand and a small gift came down a chute. Above: Jane Reynolds was the princess in 1936.

was dead. On the East Side, poor people went door-to-door, asking for food. The Dust Bowl of the mid-1930s badly damaged farmers in Kansas and other Plains states whose output of wheat and cattle was instrumental in the Kansas City economy. Half the 1935 wheat crop was destroyed by "dusters" in Kansas.

Through the 1930s, Kansas City's population declined. Until that point, the city's population had risen at least 23 percent in every decade since the Civil War.

In 1932, after a couple of years' hiatus, an abbreviated Santa Claus parade returned downtown. An account in *The Star* hinted at the problems that plagued the economy. "Hope, faith and jollity are in the air," the article said, despite "all the stale notes and heavy discords of want and riches side by side in a Christmas season."

Only by late in the decade could hints of a commercial revival be seen. On a mid-December Saturday in 1938, merchants reported their biggest day in at least two years. Nevertheless, Christmas day saw 7,700 people eating a free dinner at the Pendergast event on Fifth Street.

And at the new Municipal

86 CHRISTMASTIME IN KANSAS CITY

Auditorium, Christmas Day was booming for the Mayor's Christmas Tree program and present giveaway, an annual event since 1908. Eighteen thousand children filled the hall in 1938 and 1939, and in 1940 more than 20,000 jammed inside. Three thousand more milled in the hallways that year. Each child got a sack containing candy, peanuts, apples and oranges.

Before another year was out, Kansas Citians would have bigger things to worry about at the holiday season than the economic downturn. By Christmas 1941, their country again was at war.

A new world stuggle

As much as secular things had dominated Christmas seasons in the two decades since the last war, religion asserted itself in the wake of Pearl Harbor. Christmas 1941 arrived only 18 days after Japanese forces bombed the U.S. naval base in Hawaii. That year, Christmas Eve services taxed the capacity of Kansas City area cathedrals and churches.

At midnight mass at the Cathedral of the Immaculate Conception, Bishop Edwin V. O'Hara said of the crisis:

A clanking mechanical Santa, 6 feet high sitting, entertained passersby from his perch in a Grand Avenue display window of Emery, Bird, Thayer. As a recording cycled from a chuckle to a deep laugh, the synchronized Santa threw back his head and arms.

1919-1945: DRESSED IN HOLIDAY STYLE

THE FAMILY REUNION, AS MUCH AN INSTITUTION, AS THE CHRISTMAS TREE.

The panoply of the family Christmas get-together, as envisioned by artist Dale Beronius of *The Star* in 1938.

"With an impiety never dared in the days of paganism, whole nations have declared war on God himself. Mankind has set out to destroy itself.

"We must turn to the Christ child .... There is a little babe in a manger in far-off Bethlehem, and here and now the rush of bombers and the Panzer columns and the earth shakes with the march of scores of millions of men. Christianity proclaims that the little babe directs the destiny of mankind notwithstanding that such mighty forces are on the march."

At Grace and Holy Trinity Cathedral, people had to be turned away for lack of room.

"We must renounce the unhappy divisions of pre-war days," said Bishop Robert Nelson Spencer. "Let not bitterness go with what we must give, or give up, or do, or be in the course of this war."

On Christmas day, an interdenominational group of

religious leaders broadcast a call to Kansas Citians to pause at noon each day until the war ended for a silent prayer for victory.

"This is a struggle between the revived paganism and barbarism of antiquity and the everlasting truths of religious idealism," said Rabbi Samuel S. Mayerberg. "While on this day of peace and goodwill our hearts yearn for peace on earth, we must clearly realize that peace ... can come only when justice has triumphed over injustice, when mercy supplants brutality, when freedom prevails over bondage, when love triumphs over hate."

Joining Mayerberg were Bishops O'Hara and Spencer.

The country already had begun to feel that life would be different.

Southwestern Bell gave notice that long-distance calls on Christmas — all handled by human operators — would be delayed even more than normal because of increased use of phone lines by defense agencies.

And one mother sent a poignant letter to the editor of *The Star*, telling of how her son already was "in an army camp being prepared for no one knows what."

"Only a few short years ago, my

"Peace on earth forever, all the world together," went the words to this wartime Christmas song written and published in 1944 by J.B. Buchli of Kansas City.

1919-1945: DRESSED IN HOLIDAY STYLE

These lighthearted cards were produced by Hall Bros. Inc. in the 1940s. *Facing page*: On a more serious note, Kansas City's Siegrist Engraving Co. depicted wartime travelers in Union Station in 1942.

little son walked by my side as we went Christmas shopping," she wrote. "He was only a toddler during the other World War. Then I realized that a score of years ago other mothers suffered that I might be happy with my child. Now I must 'carry on,' and do it bravely.

"Surely there will come a time when parents may have their children toddle by their sides to visit Santa Claus and exult in the wonders of Christmas time with no war clouds hovering over them."

Although the mayor's Christmas party again packed Municipal Auditorium with 20,000 children, Christmas Day dinners for the poor drew far fewer than the years before.

The Pendergast dinner, in its third Christmas after the fall of the political machine, had only 500. The City Union Mission fed about 1,000 and the Helping Hand Institute 700 more.

The GI's Christmas

As the war wound on, Christmas generosity found a new objective — soldiers, sailors, Marines and others mobilized in the war effort. Many were far from home. By 1943 an estimated 10,000 members of the armed services were training in the Kansas City area as aviation cadets, radar operators and radio technicians. Many thousands more came through Union Station each day.

On Christmas night 1943, service men and women from all over the country danced with Kansas Citians at Municipal Auditorium. The crowd was estimated at 9,500. The program featured the magician Blackstone, Harry Kaufmann's orchestra, D'Artega's all-woman

M. Brenton — War-time travel – Kansas City – 1942

orchestra and the Adorables chorus-line group.

The show-stealer was a singer named Yvette. Just back from a tour of military camps in Europe, she brought down the house with a song she said she had "picked up" in London. It was, "I'm Going to Get Lit Up When the Lights Go Up in London."

The USO, the Service Men's Club and the Kansas City Canteen were stocked with Christmas Day treats, and many GIs who were between trains were transported from Union Station to homes of Kansas Citians for dinner. At the Paseo Service Men's Club on 18th Street, Chauncey Downs' orchestra played while turkey and chicken dinners were furnished to 1,200 servicemen.

Peace was achieved in 1945 with Allied victories in Europe and the Pacific. Troops began returning to the United States, and once-rare goods began returning to store shelves. As the war dragged on, the government had imposed limits — rationing — on goods deemed essential to the war effort, such as gasoline, coffee, soap, shoes, and copper.

In late November 1945, at the

Take it easy, civilians: These were the messages for telephone users and railroad travelers during the war.

V-Mail (for Victory Mail) kept members of the armed services in touch with home. This message came from overseas to Kansas City in 1944.

Kansas City entertained the soldiers who were stationed in town for training in radio and other modern technologies. This dinner was thrown by the Three-Star Club in December 1943.

beginning of Christmas shopping season, women were noticed lined three deep at a department-store counter downtown.

"What's the attraction over there?" a man asked.

"Rayon hose," a department manager answered. "Rayon hose."

Elsewhere in the store, a staff sergeant wearing a discharge emblem on his uniform tried on a hat while his wife looked on. He squared himself up in front of a mirror, snapped the brim down, and turned to the clerk.

"It makes me look like a cowboy," he said. "Let me see something else."

Homecoming

In the days before Christmas 1945, tens of thousands of GIs scrambled to return home. More than 150,000 were stranded on the West Coast despite the government's requisitioning trains for them. Meanwhile, civilians ignored government requests that they stay home during the shortage of passenger seats.

On Dec. 22, an official at Union Station called it "the worst night I ever spent." Two hundred servicemen holding tickets for the 2 p.m. Santa Fe train to Chicago were left on the loading platform after no one departed the fully loaded train when it came through. When a Wabash train left at 4:25 p.m. for St. Louis, 100 servicemen were left behind.

Returning soldiers and sailors were supposed to receive preference over civilians, but when 200

1919-1945: DRESSED IN HOLIDAY STYLE

servicemen in Denver saw civilians allowed first onto a Kansas City-bound Missouri Pacific train, they took matters into their own hands. They got aboard, removed civilians from their seats and made them stand in the aisles as the train pulled out. Military police understood.

"All those soldiers want is to get home for Christmas," one MP said. "Anybody who interferes with that desire is going to be set aside by the soldiers themselves."

Even the commander in chief had trouble getting home.

Harry S. Truman of Independence, sworn in as president in April after the death of Franklin Roosevelt, was delayed at the Washington airport by rain and sleet. The presidential plane encountered bad weather and heavy headwinds over Ohio, delaying Truman's arrival at the Municipal Air Terminal in Kansas City until 4:50 p.m. Christmas Day. About 150 people greeted him at the airport, some shouting, "Merry Christmas." The Secret Service and U.S. marshals cleared a path through the crowd to a black sedan where his wife, Bess Truman, and daughter, Margaret Truman, were waiting.

After a side trip to his mother's home in Grandview, the presidential party arrived at their home in Independence. Not long afterward a truck carrying a piano stopped on Delaware Street. About 75 members of the Messiah chorus of the Reorganized Church of Jesus Christ of Latter-Day Saints gathered around the truck, where their director accompanied them in the "Hallelujah Chorus" and "It Came Upon a Midnight Clear." The president came out, thanked the director and returned inside.

After a decade and a half of depression followed by war, the president and the country were ready for peace and prosperity. They would get a strange kind of peace, a cold war with outbreaks of hot war. But the prosperity would be unlike anything they could have imagined.

Toys of the times: Comic books starring superheroes such as Captain Marvel developed spinoffs such as this 1940 toy set.

Local carolers, accompanied by a truckbed piano, serenaded President Truman on Christmas Day 1945 outside his home, top left. The president cleaned his glasses as the songs were completed; his daughter, Margaret Truman, stood at the door.

The next day, Truman left to take presents to his mother and sister in Grandview, top right. In the parlor of his home on Delaware Street stood a decorated 16-foot fir tree from Colorado, which had to be trimmed to fit in the house.

1919-1945: DRESSED IN HOLIDAY STYLE

Cuddles and Tuckie save Santa's lost reindeer!

For the holiday season of 1941, children in the Kansas City area could listen to their very own 14-part radio serial, the "Christmas Adventures of Cuddles and Tuckie." Produced at WDAF radio and broadcast at 6:30 p.m. every Monday, Wednesday and Friday evening beginning Nov. 24, the program tracked two intrepid youngsters enlisted by Santa Claus to find and return his reindeer.

As the story unfolded, Dasher, Dancer and the rest of the reindeer were attacked by a wolf one night at Santa's workshop in "Lapland." Although Santa's night watchman killed the wolf, the frightened reindeer stampeded. Only a white reinder, White King, knew where Santa's team went, but none of Santa's helpers would ride him to track them down.

Cuddles and Tuckie weren't afraid. One night, White King appeared in the back yard of their suburban home. They climbed on the white reindeer's back and flew off to the frozen North. There, inside a mountain that opened as they descended from the sky, were Santa's reindeer. Riding White King, Cuddles and Tuckie drove the team back to Santa's workshop in time for Christmas.

And on Christmas Eve 1941, sandwiched between "News of the World" and "Easy Aces" on WDAF, the

Cuddles and Tuckie on White King.

"Christmas Adventures of Cuddles and Tuckie" ended with the young heroes helping Santa pack. Then they climbed aboard his sleigh and rode with him on his journey taking gifts to all the world's children.

The radio program, which returned to WDAF for six holiday seasons, was the brainchild of Frances Royster Williams, a freelance commercial artist who lived in Westwood Hills. She had invented Cuddles and Tuckie as characters in a cartoon-and-verse feature published Sundays in *The Kansas City Star* since 1932. The characters' yearlong adventures and misadventures were based on the activities of Williams' children and their playmates. Some episodes of the comic were simple, day-to-day events. Others were grander; there was a series on Easter and a meeting with British royalty. For the Christmas episodes, it was an easy leap from the newspaper pages to the broadcasts of WDAF, which was owned by the Kansas City Star Co. The Junior League, the University of Kansas City and the Kansas City Junior College helped in the productions.

The print version of Cuddles and Tuckie, which was syndicated to other newspapers, continued in *The Star* until 1960.

Memories

These people spent their childhoods in the 1920s, 1930s or early 1940s in the Kansas City area. Interviewed in 1985 for a Kansas City Museum oral history project, they recalled what was special about Christmas when they were young.

"Everybody used to get together at one person's house. They used to strike up that Victrola and wind it up and put a record on there. Everybody used to have such a good time just dancing and eating. It seem like it was a pretty good way of celebrating, you know?"

— *Frank Pisciotta (born in 1916), on growing up at 655 Park Ave.*

* * *

"My dad and mother thought that Christmas … gifts should be something of yourself, so they helped us make things. My dad being in the lumber business, lumber was cheap or he could bring it home for us. One year I made letter-holders for all my grandparents and aunts and uncles out of three pieces of wood. My dad marked it off on the lumber and let me use a small saw to cut them out. Then we had to sand them down and varnish them.

"We always had a big Christmas program at the church and Santa always came. My dad … was Santa. We didn't see why he had to be Santa — why Santa really couldn't come himself. But Mom explained to us that all the churches were having Christmas parties and, of course, Santa couldn't go to every one. So Dad had the red suit and the beard and everything. We would look at each other and grin because we knew something the rest of the youngsters didn't."

— *Virginia Staats Peterson (born 1919).*

* * *

"The Christmas *Las Posadas* … That was where you carried from door to door the Blessed Mother, Joseph and the Baby, knocking on doors to see if they would let you come in for the night … You ask for refuge, because the Blessed Mother was going to have Jesus."

— *Maria Cruz Loya (born in 1928), on growing up on the West Side.*

* * *

"There was always the Christmas program at the Methodist church. Little Catholic children that we were, we were always in the Methodist plays. All the children got to take home these wonderful little net stockings full of little treasures. We would all come home and get ready for midnight Mass. It was really a double whammy of religion!"

— *Mary Lou Holt (born 1932), on growing up in Grandview.*

* * *

"I think I knew when I was quite young that there was no Santa Claus. Believe me, it was not a shock like the psychologists like you to think. It's a game that I think the child and parent play. We'd look up in the sky and imagine if we could see Santa Claus flying by. It was just a fun game.

"The anticipation, of course, is as much as anything. The waiting and the looking-forward-to — that's probably the biggest part of it."

— *Virginia R. Taylor (born in 1933) on her childhood in Independence and Kansas City.*

1946-2000s

All our Christmases

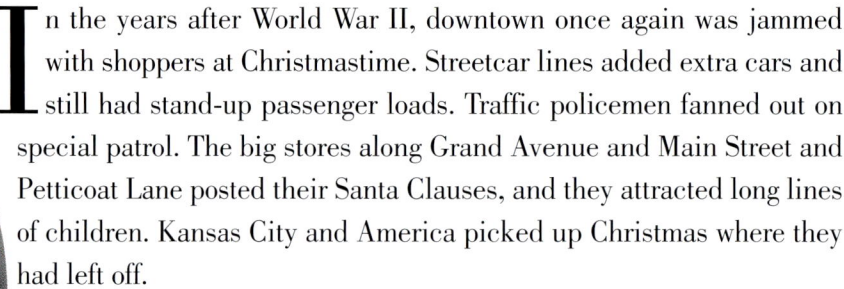

I n the years after World War II, downtown once again was jammed with shoppers at Christmastime. Streetcar lines added extra cars and still had stand-up passenger loads. Traffic policemen fanned out on special patrol. The big stores along Grand Avenue and Main Street and Petticoat Lane posted their Santa Clauses, and they attracted long lines of children. Kansas City and America picked up Christmas where they had left off.

Yet in the years to come Christmas would undergo profound changes wrought by the pressures and the pleasures of the postwar world.

Those children who queued up to visit department-store Santas were the vanguard of the baby boom, the largest generation in American history. More and more, they came from homes in subdivisions that lay far from downtown stores. And they were making unusual requests. In 1949, one store Santa reported a notable increase in pleas for television sets and combination radio-phonographs.

In the second half of the 20th century, Kansas City's Christmas would be molded by this swirl of demographic and technological change. Traditional Christmas customs lived on, but the holiday would pervade our lives as never before.

With the kids in mind

In 1947, downtown merchants sensed change in the wind. They had scheduled the area's Christmas light display to be turned on the Monday after Thanksgiving, but as the date grew closer they realized that shoppers weren't waiting that long. So on the Saturday after Thanksgiving, two nights earlier than planned, 14,000 red, yellow, blue and green lights flashed on. Even that was late, as it turned out. Officials of the merchants association estimated that the

Midcentury baubles and bulb.
Facing page: **The shopping season began in earnest the day after Thanksgiving 1959 on 11th Street — Petticoat Lane.**

1946-2000s: ALL OUR CHRISTMASES

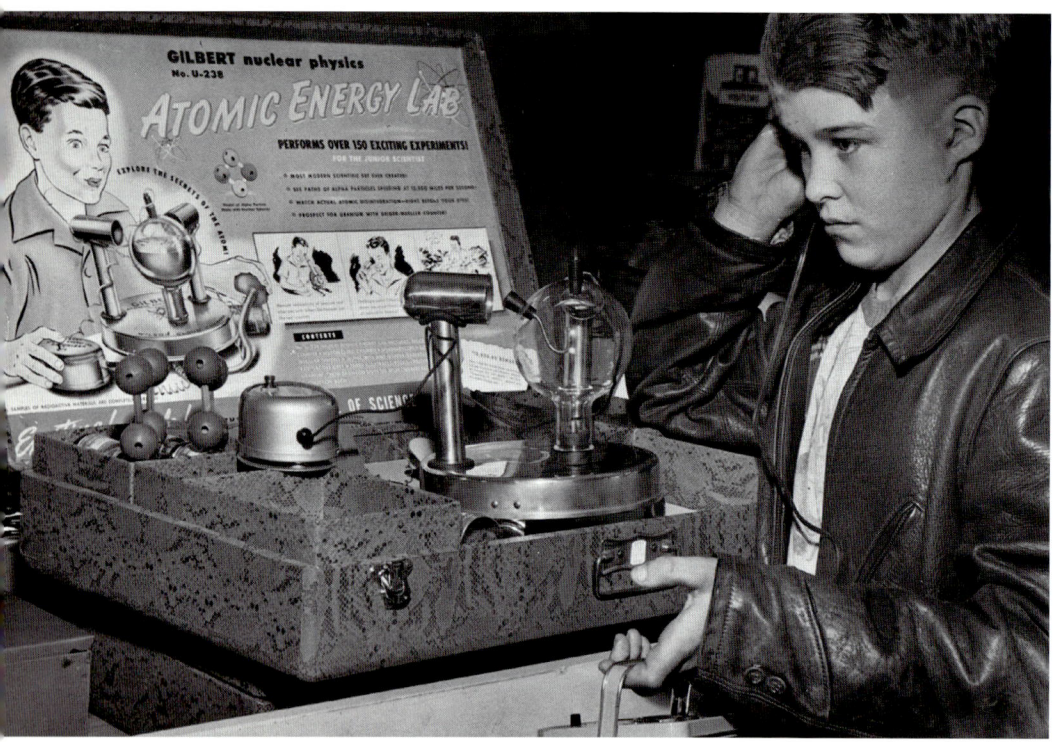

In the early days of the Atomic Age, one toy company offered an Atomic Energy Lab, complete with geiger counter. This 12-year-old checked it out at a downtown Kansas City department store in mid-December 1950.

This early '60s Christmas dress was made for a Kansas City, Kan., girl by her mother.

managers: toys.

Children had long been the center of the Christmas celebration. The tree, the presents, Santa Claus — all existed primarily for them. Now there were going to be more children than ever.

Beginning in 1946 and continuing for almost two decades, 76 million babies were born in the United States. By 1947, gifts for these baby-boom children dominated Christmas advertising.

At the Jones Store on 12th between Main and Walnut streets, trains were big: Toy electric trains for presents and a miniature Burlington Zephyr ride for entertainment. The same was true a block away at Emery, Bird, Thayer's Toy Town, which also offered toy sewing machines, and baby dolls and board games.

Sears Roebuck and Co. pushed tricycles and dolls, also listing wagons, scooters, doll buggies and toy wheelbarrows. And as of 1947 Sears had added a big new Kansas City location — the Country Club Plaza.

Where the shopping is easy

Since its inception in the 1920s, the Plaza had drawn shoppers to its variety of stores, many of them

Friday after Thanksgiving had been the heaviest in November history.

Shoppers in 1947 found that manufacturers had begun to shake off wartime restrictions. Refrigerators, toy trains, dolls, kitchen ranges, wool blankets and hundreds of other products in short supply during the war were showing up on shelves.

One category of goods moved with speed that astounded store

Sacks of Christmas mail were stacked high on wagons that lined platforms at Union Station in December 1957.

upscale. Holidays were an important time for sales, and on the Plaza seasonal decorations were a specialty. At Easter, bunny statues were set out; in the autumn big jack-o'-lanterns and a witch house appeared.

Of these efforts, the greatest by far was the Christmas display of electric lights.

In 1947 the Plaza lights were switched on the night after Thanksgiving and promptly drew crowds of sightseeing motorists so large that the city had to alter traffic patterns on streets nearby during the shopping season. Four extra policemen were on duty the night the lights went on, and eight the next night to route automobiles that streamed through the area.

In 1949, the Plaza arranged for a chorus to sing carols.

"Bring the kiddies to see the Plaza's lights — It's a real Christmas treat!" an advertisement said. "Enjoy soft Christmas carol music every night on the Plaza from 7:30 p.m. to 9 p.m. (except Sundays)."

In its publicity, the Plaza listed its advantages:

■ "Convenient free parking within a block of any store."

■ "Exciting modern shops."

This Christmas lighting kit featured standard lights and modern bubble lights.

This midcentury suburban panorama of single-family homes, winding lanes, automobiles and children at play was conceived by artist Dale Beronius for *The Star* of Christmas Eve 1950.

■ "Leisurely gift selections free from the aggravation of huge crowds and traffic snarls."

"Make your shopping for Christmas *easy* this year," was the pitch.

The point was to contrast the Plaza with the bustle of downtown, and the point was hitting home.

In 1950, the Plaza drew a throng of children and parents for the dedication of a 10-foot replica of Rudolph, the Red-Nosed Reindeer, in a lot on 47th Street near Wornall Road. Machinery to make Rudolph's tail wag and his nose glow red was set in motion the night of Nov. 30 by the writer of the Rudolph story, Robert May. The display also featured a 30-minute tape recording of Christmas songs by Gene Autry, the cowboy singer whose version of "Rudolph, the Red-Nosed Reindeer" was a hit.

That was only part of it. A

strolling Santa Claus patroled the area near Rudolph the last two weeks before Christmas. Meanwhile, 30,000 Christmas lights and 28 white-painted evergreens marked the roof lines and other areas of Plaza buildings.

By 1954 the Plaza had made the switching-on of the lights an occasion unto itself. That year, it enlisted the Robert Shaw Chorale, in town for a concert at the Music Hall, and the choir of Village Presbyterian Church to accompany a lighting ceremony at 7 p.m. the Friday after Thanksgiving. Hundreds of people gathered in the triangular park east of the Plaza Theatre. Robert Shaw switched on the lights in a life-size creche nearby and on a tree in the park, and then the rest of the lights were turned on, block by block. The program, organized by the Kansas City Council of Churches, had a religious theme.

The next year the Plaza lighting was seen across the country. NBC television's evening news program — anchored by former Kansas City journalist John Cameron Swayze — gave the lighting two minutes of airtime the night after Thanksgiving. Randall Jessee of WDAF-TV described the scene for an estimated six to eight million NBC viewers. By then the lights were said to number 50,000 and to be strung over 30 miles of wire. Central Street was blocked off, and the crowd that gathered was

Wired for Christmas

The lights on the Country Club Plaza and throughout downtown were turned on simultaneously the night before Thanksgiving in 1952 — as part of the magic of televison.

WDAF television produced a one-hour Christmas special, "Christmas Comes to Kansas City." In the closing skit a little girl dreamed of being in Santa's workshop and pointing out how important electronics were to modern life. She produced a special electrical switch, which Santa pressed. With help from Kansas City Power & Light Co., the lights in both retail districts popped on at the same moment.

In 1950, this house on Canterbury Street in Fairway won a prize in a Junior Chamber of Commerce home lighting contest. Below: For baby-boom children, a toy version of a 1957 Ford was a dream come true.

Downtown turned its lights on the night after Thanksgiving 1955 to try to compete with outlying shopping districts

estimated at 3,000. When the switch was thrown that night in 1955, some of the relays failed; the displays on some buildings flashed on, then flickered off, then back on. Producers kept television cameras pointed at the live lights.

There were other competitors for the lighting tradition. Merchants along Troost between 31st Street and Linwood Boulevard turned on their lighting display the same night. North Kansas City and Independence merchants staged lighting displays, too.

All were aimed at increasing Christmas shopping business. All over town, stores now were staying open until 8:30 or 9 p.m. nightly from mid-December until just before Christmas, some even beginning the night after Thanksgiving.

The ease of shopping away from downtown was becoming attractive — particularly for residents of the new suburbs.

The sprawling city

Downtown merchants understood their problem. In 1955, the same year the Plaza lighting appeared on national television, building and store owners downtown lighted their structures one by one at 30-second intervals until the area was ablaze. City Hall and the Kansas City

Power & Light Co. skyscraper were among them. The lighting was staged by a promotional group called Downtown Unlimited in an attempt to attract shoppers.

Amateur photographers gathered on the Liberty Memorial hill to record what some described as the effect of a cluster of jewels. A camera store offered two new cameras to the best color and the best black-and-white pictures of the scene.

During shopping hours, downtown merchants arranged for Christmas carols to be played over loudspeakers. Extra city buses were scheduled to carry people to and fro, and a car dealer on 18th Street near Baltimore Avenue inaugurated a shuttle service. Shoppers could park on the dealer's lot south of downtown and get a free ride in a "Christmas-red Chrysler or Plymouth" to the big department stores.

But downtown was swimming against a tidal wave.

After World War II tens of thousands of returning service men and women, taking advantage of government programs to go to college and to buy homes, began raising families. And those families increasingly moved to new housing in neighborhoods that sprang up on the urban fringe. Acre after acre was filled with single-family homes with lawns and garages and driveways.

Getting there and back was eased by a boom in highway construction — particularly four-lane highways. Initially, planners believed those highways would help speed traffic into and around downtown. In the end, they did a better job taking people away.

Soon subdivisions were gathered into cities — Prairie Villages and Gladstones and Fairways and Raytowns. Kansas City itself began gobbling up hundreds of square miles, many of them north of the Missouri River. Kansas City,

At a Kansas City Christmas party, December 1954.

1946-2000s: ALL OUR CHRISTMASES

In 1959, greenery crossed streets for the first time since the removal of power lines for streetcars and trolley buses, left. At each intersection hung an oversize lantern. In the early 1960s, colorful lighted crowns were placed above intersections, below right, this one on Walnut Street. By 1972, the crowns were airier and bore more tinsel than ever, below left.

Facing page: Petticoat Lane at night, early 1960s.

1946-2000s: ALL OUR CHRISTMASES

Sign of the times: In 1949, Billie Brown was Kline's Fairy Princess at its store downtown, left. By 1966, Kline's had opened a branch store in the Ward Parkway Shopping Center, where Carla Cooper greeted children, above, and one at Antioch Center in the Northland.

Kan., followed suit, as did Independence.

As the metropolitan area sprawled outward, retailers followed.

The Prairie Village Shopping Center opened in 1948, three years before the city was formed. In 1956, Antioch Shopping Center opened with 34 shops at Antioch and Vivion Roads in Kansas City, North. The next year, Truman Corners' 39 shops opened near Grandview.

In fall 1958, an even bigger shopping district came along, the Blue Ridge Shopping Center in Independence. Along State Line Road, the first retail operations of the Ward Parkway Shopping Center began in 1959; by 1961 the center with its enclosed mall was open for several businesses. In the 1960s, 95th Street and Metcalf Avenue in Johnson County was transformed from an intersection of two-lane rural highways into a shopping behemoth. The French Market Shopping Center opened on the northeast corner in 1963, and four years later Metcalf South, an enclosed mall, began operations on the southeast corner.

Huge new shopping centers and malls continued to sprout into the 1970s: Indian Springs in 1971 in Kansas City, Kan.; Independence Center in 1974; Oak Park in 1975 and Metro North in 1976. Million-square-foot shopping centers dotted the metro area. As each of them opened, subordinate strip malls opened nearby.

Retailing in downtown Kansas City — and also in downtown Kansas City, Kan. — withered.

A two-block stretch of Walnut Street illustrated the change. In 1950, from 11th Street to 13th Street, the area contained entrances to two major department stores — Kline's and the Jones Store — and 26 other retail operations: Six women's clothing stories; three jewelers; a cafeteria; candy store; drug store; music store; paint store; optometrist; florist and others. The number dropped slightly in 1960.

By 1970, an auto parking garage had taken the place of several storefronts, and by 1980 the number of street-level retailers in those two blocks had plummeted to five.

The parking lots of the 4-year-old Blue Ridge Shopping Center in Independence were jammed with the cars of Christmas shoppers in December 1962. Interstate 70 was under construction on the mall's north side.

Despite the rapid decline in the number of retail stores downtown, a few large retailers held on. These shoppers were waiting for a bus at 11th and Main Streets in 1973.

A battle lost

In the early 1960s, merchants hung ever grander and more colorful Christmas displays over downtown intersections. And from 1963 to 1966 they sponsored a late-November Christmas parade. Scores of huge balloons, reminiscent of those in Macy's Thanksgiving Day parade in New York, were guided by Boy Scouts and joined by area high school marching bands, a Santa Claus character, clowns and elephants.

Yet nothing stemmed the retail flight.

Perhaps the most striking departure from downtown was the closing of Emery, Bird, Thayer. The massive store had been a landmark on the north side of 11th Street between Walnut and Grand Avenue for more than seven decades. Its show windows were covered by an arched palisade that protected browsers and passersby from inclement weather. Emery, Bird, Thayer shut its doors in midsummer 1968, bringing a stunning end to a shopping tradition that at Christmastime had featured Toy Town and a huge mechanical Santa in a display window. The store also had devoted employees, who staged annual reunion picnics for years after the closing.

The symbolic swan song of downtown Christmas shopping came in 1982. As workers strung lights on the Country Club Plaza that September, the head of a downtown merchants group said he doubted he could raise the $30,000 necessary to install lights for the Christmas season. Retailing had declined severely, and the remaining businesses were reluctant to contribute.

"I wouldn't contribute," said a barber whose shop was on 10th Street, "People don't shop downtown anyway."

The sad news inspired about $10,000 in last-minute contributions, so some of the lights were put up one last time. Nevertheless, nine huge, lighted crowns that had been suspended over intersections remained in storage. Installing them required four buildings at each intersection for support; by 1982 all except one of the intersections where they traditionally hung had vacant corners.

After that year, the downtown lights did not return.

Where better?

In 1957, the head of the Country Club Plaza Association of merchants boldly asked, "Where better could Christmas season for the whole world begin?"

That year former President Harry S. Truman stood on a balcony at 312 W. 47th St. and threw the switch, saying, "Let's prove to the world that we're proud to be living in

This 7-year-old had a lot to tell Santa about in 1971.

The Lennon Sisters were a popular act on Lawrence Welk's musical TV show. This 1950s paper-doll kit was a companion item.

1946-2000s: ALL OUR CHRISTMASES

The downtown Christmas parade, an off-an-on event from 1929 into the middle 1930s, was staged again by merchants in the 1960s. Thousands watched the nighttime spectacle, which featured inflated balloon figures.
Facing page: A monkey figure rode a bulldog as it was guided by Boy Scouts at the corner of Main Street and Petticoat Lane.

1946-2000s: ALL OUR CHRISTMASES

Hallmark cards

A sampling of Christmas cards produced since the 1950s by Kansas City's Hallmark, the world's biggest greeting-card maker. For some cards, the company commissioned celebrities to design covers.

The '50s

The '60s

The '70s

CHRISTMASTIME IN KANSAS CITY

The '80s

Cards by notables

Winston Churchill

Grandma Moses

Jane Wyman

Saul Steinberg

Norman Rockwell

Henry Fonda

Groucho Marx

Fred MacMurray

CHRISTMASTIME IN KANSAS CITY   115

Mayor Ilus W. Davis, in the dark coat in front of a crowd estimated at more than 30,000, switched on the Plaza Christmas lights on Thanksgiving night 1969.

the heart of America." Airliners were encouraged to fly over the Plaza area once the lights were on, and pilots for TWA, Continental, Braniff and United received statistics about the lights to read to passengers.

By 1960 tens of thousands of spectators headed to the Plaza each year to watch the lighting ceremony, which by then occurred regularly on Thanksgiving night. Police estimates of the total varied widely, but by late in the decade the number 30,000 was considered fairly firm. The estimate of light bulbs used by the end of the 1960s numbered almost 100,000. By the middle of the 1970s, the announced number was raised to 150,000 connected by an estimated 38 miles of wiring.

Mayors Ilus Davis and Charles Wheeler (who in 1972 wore a Santa Claus costume) — even the mayor of Seville, Spain, by long distance — helped in the ceremonial switch-throwing. Foreign exchange students, Disney and Worlds of Fun characters, Royals' star George Brett, FBI Director Clarence M. Kelley, various local choirs and a stream of local and state politicians joined as the years went by.

Spectators jammed sidewalks and streets, and lined rooftops and balconies. Once the Alameda Plaza Hotel was constructed on the south side of Brush Creek in the 1970s, it became a favorite vantage point for the ceremony; rooms were reserved

The Plaza lights: How they're done

Installation of the Plaza lights begins in September. The lights are finally tested in the wee hours of the Wednesday before Thanksgiving; defective bulbs and circuits are spotted and fixed. The lights are extinguished after New Year's, and in the next three months workers remove, test and fix them for the next year.

Taking count

By 1981, the Plaza Association was stating that 152,000 light bulbs were used for the annual display. Electricians whose task it was to install them, speaking with a *Kansas City Times* reporter, cautiously hinted at a question about that number.

"We sat down and counted them," one said. And how many were there? "I'm not going to say," he replied. "Whatever they say is close enough," another electrician said, not wanting to stir up anything with the Plaza Association.

Helping string lights in the last days before Thanksgiving 1990 was Ivan Hendrickson.

The crowd roared its approval in 1980 as Royals' star George Brett helped throw the light switch for the second time. That year he won his second batting championship and the Royals made their first trip to the World Series.

Students at Pembroke-Country Day, Barstow and Sunset Hill schools composed the 180-member choir for the 1969 lighting ceremony.

But if you hum a few bars...

In autumn 1976, the Kansas City Royals were the hottest item in town, having recently won the city's first Major League Baseball championship of any kind — the American League's Western Division. Their stars were George Brett and Hal McRae, who had battled each other for the league batting championship to the last day of the regular season. Brett won and, perhaps as a result, was chosen to switch on the Plaza lights on Thanksgiving night.

Standing before an adoring and cheering throng at the Plaza, Brett said that all he wanted for Christmas was to reach the World Series in 1977. He added that this was his first Thanksgiving away from his family in California, and that it was time to turn on the lights. However, master of ceremonies Larry Moore of KMBC-TV was told by Plaza Association officials that the moment would have to wait until precisely 8 p.m., so Moore tried to gain a few minutes' time.

"First let's whip up a little spirit," he announced. "Let's sing 'Jingle Bells.' What do you think of that, George?"

"I don't know the words," he replied.

Undaunted, Moore led the crowd in three round of Jingle Bells and then began the 10-second countdown, at the end of which he, Brett and a Santa Claus character pressed the switch and the lights came on.

CHRISTMASTIME IN KANSAS CITY

1946-2000s: ALL OUR CHRISTMASES

Off in a crisis, then back on

In 1973, when the Organization of Petroleum Exporting Countries clamped down on world oil supplies and energy became a national concern, the Plaza delivered a local thunderbolt by extinguishing its lights in the midst of the Christmas shopping season.

On the evening of Nov. 25, President Richard Nixon in a televised address called for a ban on Sunday sales of gasoline, reduced speed limits and the rationing of heating oil. Nixon also asked Americans to eliminate decorative outdoor lighting. Within an hour Miller Nichols, chairman of the board of the J.C. Nichols Co., ordered the Plaza lights turned off. That took place only three days after their ceremonial turning-on.

> "We will actually burn less electricity with the lights on than off."
>
> — *Miller Nichols, chairman of the J.C. Nichols Co.*

A little more than two weeks later, Nichols relented. On Dec. 13 the lights were turned back on. The fact that Nixon planned to join in lighting the national Christmas tree on the White House lawn, Nichols said, meant the president surely approved of some outdoor lighting. Nichols said the Plaza would use less electricity with the Christmas lights on, anyway, because their use removed the need for brighter and more energy-intensive security lights. As a reminder of the energy crisis, however, their nightly hours of illumination were restricted to 6 p.m. to 9 p.m. and they would be turned off for good after Christmas Day, an earlier end than customary.

months in advance. The nearby Raphael, after it was opened as a hotel, had the same crush of requests.

Whatever the precise number of people or bulbs, there was no doubt that the Plaza lighting ceremony was fixed as the Christmas season-beginning tradition, not only for Kansas City but also for the entire region. It became the community Christmas symbol.

Once the Thanksgiving ceremony was over, the Plaza settled into its accustomed role of upscale shopping district — albeit the region's best known. Its popularity symbolized what had become a snowballing effect on the American retail economy, and consequently on the public Christmas. Downtown had once drawn people together from all over to spend money on Christmas gifts. Now, that community Christmas — commercial as it was — was scattered to all corners of the area.

Customs, enduring and new

As the years went by, Kansas City's public Christmas carried on in the Plaza lighting celebration, in the decorations and events at every shopping mall, and in displays at parks.

Encouraged by contests, home decorations became extravagant through the 1950s and the 1960s. A home in Kansas City, North, won a prize in 1950, above. A Raytown winner, below right, had carolers, "Peanuts" characters and others in 1962.

Santa drove and Frosty the Snowman was the footman on a full-size stagecoach, part of the decorations on a Kansas City home in 1967, left.

1946-2000s: ALL OUR CHRISTMASES

Other Kansas City Christmas traditions changed with the times, but survived. In 1955, Mayor H. Roe Bartle ended the annual Mayor's Christmas Tree party for children, the party that began in 1908 at Convention Hall and moved to Municipal Auditorium in the 1930s, drawing upwards of 20,000 in some years. Attendance declined after World War II, so Bartle redirected the effort toward raising money for multiple projects — gift certificates for the poor and the elderly, Toys for Tots distributions, and Santa's Wonderland at Gillham Park and in Kansas City, North. In 1990 alone the Mayors' Christmas Tree Association sponsored 78 Christmas parties for more than 20,000 children in

The Mayor's Christmas Tree stood in Gillham Park in 1967 beside a city-sponsored Nativity scene, above. Next to them was Santa's Wonderland, a temporary playground with a Christmas theme, left.

community centers, hospitals and YMCAs. By the end of the 20th century, the fund was assisting as many as 30,000 people through more than $100,000 in donations.

The site of the big community tree was moved from near Union Station to Gillham Park, and finally in 1973 to the plaza at Crown Center. There the tree was lighted, usually on the Friday after Thanksgiving, by succeeding mayors and celebrities such as golfer Tom Watson, sprinter Maurice Green, baseball raconteur Buck O'Neil and Chiefs football players Joe Montana and Marcus Allen. In recent years, the tree — sometimes reaching 100 feet tall and typically labeled the tallest Christmas tree in the country — has been imported from Oregon. Seven thousand bulbs and more than 1,000 ornaments decorate it. Once the mayor's tree comes down after New Year's, the wood is used to craft thousands of Christmas ornaments, which are sold to benefit the fund.

As some Kansas City traditions changed, new ones sprang up.

Many cities in the metropolitan area have lighted their own Christmas trees, often referred to as mayor's trees. Among them: Kansas City,

By 1977, the mayor's tree had moved north to the plaza of Crown Center, where Royals' manager Whitey Herzog helped in the lighting ceremony.

At the malls

Christmas shopping at malls became typical as the giant retail complexes sprang up across the Kansas City metropolitan area in the 1970s. Waiting at benches was a common experience for teenagers, left in 1980, as well as husbands and boyfriends, above in 1979. Those still afoot jammed the escalators and corridors, facing page, in 1987.

CHRISTMASTIME IN KANSAS CITY   125

Facing page: **At 91 years of age, Don Jacobson of Kansas City was still volunteering as a bell ringer at Ward Parkway Shopping Center in 1988.** *Above:* **A Salvation Army brass quartet played at 12th and Main in 1971, seeking donations. The results came when army members delivered packages, below.**

Kan., Independence, Olathe, Harrisonville, Lee's Summit, Belton and Shawnee.

Each year, the Salvation Army in Kansas City, and in other cities across the country, puts up its Tree of Lights, marking the beginning of its red-kettle Christmas charity fund-raising campaign.

Jackson County and Johnson County parks departments have staged Christmas lighting displays for motorists to drive through. Historic homes, sites and buildings are decorated with Christmas themes.

In 1980, the Missouri Repertory Theatre began annual productions of Charles Dickens' "A Christmas Carol,"

1946-2000s: ALL OUR CHRISTMASES

A sadness on Christmas

As wags have been fond of saying for years, Dec. 25, 1971, was the day the Grinch stole Christmas — from fans of the Kansas City Chiefs.

On that unseasonably warm holiday Saturday afternoon, more than 50,000 people jammed Municipal Stadium at 22nd Street and Brooklyn Avenue to watch a National Football League playoff game between the Chiefs and the Miami Dolphins. In the days beforehand, there had been complaints about the NFL's timing. Some newspaper columnists around the country called it a desecration of the holiday. One Kansas City family announced it was tearing up its tickets, and a Platte County state representative threatened to introduce a bill prohibiting games on Christmas in the state.

But the game went on — and on and on, through two overtimes. Near the end of regulation play the Chiefs' usually reliable placekicker, Jan Stenerud, missed an easy field-goal attempt that would have won the game for Kansas City. Another was blocked in the first overtime; it, too, would have won the game. The score stood 24-24 until Miami's placekicker, Garo Ypremian, completed a 37-yard field goal. The crowd watched in a tomblike silence. Final score: Miami 27, Kansas City 24. It was the longest game in NFL history at 82 minutes and 40 seconds.

As the fans filed quietly from the game, the last professional football game played in Municipal Stadium, Stenerud told the media:

"I have the worst feeling anyone could have. I feel like hiding. It's unbearable. It's totally unbearable."

Jan Stenerud hung his head after the Miami Dolphins blocked his attempt at the game-winning field goal.

Humbug! For seven years in the 1990s, Gary Holcombe played Ebenezer Scrooge in Missouri Repertory Theatre's "A Christmas Carol."

which have proved popular not only with Kansas Citians but also with busloads of out-of-towners who come to see the play and hear carolers in the lobby of the Helen F. Spencer Theatre at the University of Missouri-Kansas City. Nearly 30,000 people have seen one of the performances each year.

Going national

As the second half of the 20th century unfolded, Kansas City's own Christmas customs were met, sometimes matched and occasionally overshadowed by a festival that emerged rapidly all across the country. It occurred each year, on television.

In league with manufacturers and merchants and advertisers, television networks in the 1950s began presenting stories and symbols that millions of Americans watched at once. Regular series of domestic comedies and dramatic shows featured Christmas episodes. Hourlong variety shows with Christmas themes became big, too. Often, the most popular of those presentations were repeated in later years.

Some special television

programs became traditions. One of the earliest was "Amahl and the Night Visitors," an opera by Gian Carlo Menotti commissioned by Kansas City's Hallmark cards for its first Hallmark Hall of Fame in 1951.

In 1965, "A Charlie Brown Christmas" was broadcast, based on Charles M. Shultz's "Peanuts" comic strip. In 1966 came another animated network special, "How the Grinch Stole Christmas!" from the popular 1957 book of pictures and verse by Theodore Geisel, Dr. Seuss.

National television annually brought to bigger audiences than ever a set of Christmas movies that had first appeared at mid-century. *Holiday Inn*, released in 1942, and its 1954 spinoff, *White Christmas*, were both song-filled light comedies centered on holiday lodges. *It's a Wonderful Life* of 1946 was the story of a discouraged small-town businessman who found new meaning in life at Christmastime. *Miracle on 34th Street* dealt with Santa Claus and his reality, and *The Bishop's Wife* of 1947 brought an angel to help out a minister.

Other media also helped make Christmas a nationwide event. Coca-Cola's jolly giant Santa Claus, appearing in colorful magazine ads and on billboards, became a standard depiction of what a century before was called a "right jolly old elf."

Among the Irving Berlin songs introduced in *Holiday Inn*, "White Christmas" became one of the best-selling recorded songs of all time. Yet another enduring song was "Rudolph, the Red-Nosed Reindeer," which began in 1939 as a story-poem distributed to millions of customers by Montgomery Ward. In 1947 a children's book version appeared, and in 1949 Gene Autry sang a musical version with words by Johnny Marks.

In all media, advertising brought the country news of the latest fads in gifts, particularly toys. Model trains and various dolls and electronic games all had their times of intense demand.

By the beginning of the 21st century, for Kansas City and the rest of the country, Christmas pervaded all levels of life — individual, family, church, neighborhood, city and country.

Toys of the times: A Simpsons family doll set made about 1990.

O Christmas tree! Their pine freshly cut, customers at Santa's Christmas Farm in Jackson County hitched a ride to the cashier in 1970.

Christmas on the eve of a new century

Long ago the words "Kansas City" came to encompass more than the official boundaries of the city in Missouri or the one in Kansas. As the years passed toward the end of the 20th century, a Kansas City Christmas was being celebrated from Lee's Summit to Liberty, from Independence to Edwardsville, from Platte Woods to Overland Park.

These pages of photographs and words touch on the modern Kansas City Christmas and its manifestations. From individual experiences to public extravaganzas, from the seasonal barbs of the newspaper cartoonist to a tender sentiment by Bill Vaughan, they represent a part of what has become the story of the season.

"Silent Night" by candlelight: A Christmas Eve service at First Christian Church in Bonner Springs, 1993.

1946-2000s: ALL OUR CHRISTMASES

Christmas in the Park, an annual drive-through display of lighted figures sponsored by Jackson County Parks and Recreation, in 2000.

Left: This extravaganza has decorated a Prairie Village home at Christmastime for decades. Each year, thousands of people have driven or walked by the house in the 7600 block of Falmouth Street to see the seasonal labor of love staged by Mike Babick. Since he began the display in the 1960s, Babick has spent tens of thousands of dollars, seen thousands of visitors — and faced down occasional complaints from some of his neighbors (photo from 1994).

CHRISTMASTIME IN KANSAS CITY

Opening the shopping season on the day after Thanksgiving: Teen-age girls at Oak Park Mall, 1992.

Crowds of all ages at J.C. Penney's outlet store in Overland Park, right, 1994.

Facing page: As the season neared its end, last-minute shopping was under way in 1990 at Bannister Mall in Kansas City.

1946-2000s: ALL OUR CHRISTMASES

That meeting with Santa

The jolly old elf (or one of his helpers) is everywhere at Christmas. In the 1990s he ranged from Blue Springs, left, to Antioch Center in the Northland, above, to Prairie Village, top.

Clockwise from top: In the 1980s, Santa visited a restaurant near Troost Elementary on the East Side, a party at a downtown hotel for Guadalupe Center children on the West Side, and a party for cystic fibrosis victims on the Country Club Plaza.

CHRISTMASTIME IN KANSAS CITY

1946-2000s: ALL OUR CHRISTMASES

Arriving by air

A helicopter-borne Santa landed in the parking lot of a shopping center in Shawnee in 1992, greeted children and began collecting donated toys left at a group of hardware stores.

CHRISTMASTIME IN KANSAS CITY

From the 1960s until the late '90s, a 30-foot Santa with a spiral slide inside was trucked the short distance to Santa's Wonderland in Gillham Park by Kansas City Parks and Recreation Department workers, above. Because of safety concerns, the permanent Santa was replaced by an inflatable version in 1999.

By Lee Judge in *The Star*, Dec. 12, 1997.

Next page: Plaza lighting ceremony, 1991.

Why we like the lights
"It's a euphoric, whimsical feeling that brings out the kid in everyone. It's awe. It's fascination. You're gleeful. Your entire countenance changes. It's an aura it exudes. It's wonderful."

— *Olathe resident Deborah Davis, at the Plaza lighting ceremony, mid-1990s*

1946-2000s: ALL OUR CHRISTMASES

Christmas Mass for children at Queen of the Holy Rosary Church in Overland Park, 1990.

Preparation for Christmas: Members of the Melgoza family pitching in to assemble tamales for Christmas Eve dinner on Kansas City's West Side, 1999.

1946-2000s: ALL OUR CHRISTMASES

Young members of Grace Assembly of God church waiting to perform in the congregation's Christmas pageant on Kansas City's East Side, 1999.

A neighborhood alight; the Mission Ridge subdivision in southeast Olathe, Kan., 1990.

1946-2000s: ALL OUR CHRISTMASES

Kindergartners from Spring Valley Elementary School entertaining residents of a nursing home in Raytown, 1997.

Right: The Mayor's Christmas Concert at the RLDS Auditorium in Independence, 1998, begun in 1985 to raise money for the needy.

1946-2000s: ALL OUR CHRISTMASES

The tuba Christmas concert at Town Pavilion downtown, 1993, a booming tradition since 1982.

152   CHRISTMASTIME IN KANSAS CITY

Preparing Christmas dinners for the needy at Pleasant Green Baptist Church in Kansas City, Kan., 2000. Helpers came from Congregation Beth Torah in Overland Park, Kan., and Village Presbyterian Church in Prairie Village, Kan.

I saw Santa kissing....It was all between friends at the Ward Parkway Shopping Center in December 1980.

Left: Thousands of bulbs, thousands of spectators, thousands of dollars for charity. The Mayor's Christmas Tree and the benefactions it inspires have endured since the late 1870s.

1946-2000s: ALL OUR CHRISTMASES

The Best Christmas Story of Them All

By Bill Vaughan

"Tell me a story of Christmas," she said.

The television mumbled faint inanities in the next room. From a few houses down the block came the sound of car doors slamming and guests being greeted with large cordiality.

Her father thought awhile. His mind went back over the interminable parade of Christmas books he had read at the bedsides of his children.

"Well," he started, tentatively, "once upon a time it was the week before Christmas, and all the little elves at the North Pole were sad — "

"I'm tired of elves," she whispered.

And he could tell she was tired, maybe almost as weary as he was himself after the last few feverish days.

"OK," he said. "There was once, in a city not very far from here, the cutest, wriggly little puppy you ever saw. The snow was falling, and this little puppy didn't have a home. As he walked along the streets, he saw a house that looked quite a bit like our house. And at the window — "

"Was a little girl who looked quite a bit like me," she said with a sigh. "I'm tired of puppies. I love Pinky, of course. I mean story puppies."

"OK," he said. "No puppies. This narrows the field."

"What?"

"Nothing. I'll think of something. Oh, sure. There was a forest, way up in the North, farther even than where Uncle Ed lives. And all the trees were talking about how each one was going to be the grandest Christmas tree of all. One said, 'I'm going to stand in front of

the White House where the President of the whole United States lives, and everybody will see me.'

"And another beautiful tree said, proudly, 'I am going to be in the middle of New York City and all the people will see me and think I am the most beautiful tree in the world.'

"And then a little fir tree spoke up and said, 'I am going to be a Christmas tree, too.' And all the trees laughed and laughed and said: 'A Christmas tree? You? Who would want you?' "

"No trees, Daddy," she said. "We

The first known instance of this column's publication was on the editorial page of The Kansas City Star *on Christmas Day 1960. It was reprinted occasionally after that, and for the last two decades has appeared annually in the newspaper at Christmastime. Bill Vaughan was the longtime resident humorist at* The Star, *generating the Starbeams column as well as essays for more than 30 years. At the time of his death in 1977, Vaughan was also associate editor.*

have a tree at school and at Sunday school and at the supermarket and downstairs and a little one in my room. I am very tired of trees."

"You are very spoiled," he said.

"Hmmm," she replied. "Tell me a Christmas story."

"Let's see. All the reindeer up at the North Pole were looking forward to pulling Santa's sleigh. All but one, and he felt sad because," he began with a jolly ring in his voice but quickly realized that this wasn't going to work either.

His daughter didn't say anything; she just looked at him reproachfully.

"Tired of reindeer, too?" he asked. "Frankly, so am I. How about Christmas on the farm when I was a little boy? Would you like to hear about how it was in the olden days, when my grandfather would heat up bricks and put them in the sleigh and we'd all go for a ride?"

"Yes, Daddy," she said, obediently. "But not right now. Not tonight."

He was silent, thinking. His repertoire, he was afraid, was exhausted.

She was quiet, too. Maybe, he thought, I'm home free. Maybe she has gone to sleep.

"Daddy, she murmured. "Tell me a story of Christmas."

Then it was as though he could read the words, so firmly were they in his memory. Still holding her hand, he leaned back: "And it came to pass in those days, that there went out a decree from Caesar Augustus, that all the world should be taxed .... "

Her hand tightened a bit in his, and he told her a story of Christmas.

Afterword

Christmas feelings — private ones and ones shared with others — are wrapped up in memories of occasions and people and sights and smells. Each memory is cherished in the soft focus of time's passage.

Each year those memories raise expectations for the oncoming Christmas, both for ourselves and for our community. Each year the expectations can be a struggle to match.

Shopping for gifts, as an example, can be exhilarating and frustrating all in the same trip. One moment, hustle and bustle and color and music create a joyful, shared excitement in shopping districts. The next moment, crowded streets and parking lots and walkways symbolize only delay and missed opportunities and bankbooks depleted.

Travel by public transportation spikes at Christmas, telephone lines are jammed, and mail floods post offices as cards and presents fly around the country.

Most of this activity has to do with family, close and distant. Family relationships, spotlighted in the holiday season, inevitably bring both pleasure and pain.

Loneliness, too, is highlighted at Christmas, when the rest of the world *seems* to be having such a jolly time.

The very fact that each of us in some way has to cope with Christmas proves its power, and — even setting aside religion and culture and age and social standing — its universality.

In her book, *Christmas in America*, Penne Restad took note of the annual complaint that Christmas was crumbling in the face of commerce and materialism. The complaint, of course, is at least a century old. Despite it, the Christmas spirit has survived. It lives on in our minds, she says, as a time to recall "some past moment of faith and transcendence...a metaphor for a more perfect world."

In Kansas City, as throughout America and much of the world, Christmas is a time when we look to our ideals. It's when we see whether — even in the smallest way — we can nudge the world around us a little closer to our dreams.

ACKNOWLEDGEMENTS

My deepest thanks go to the archivists, librarians and collection managers who provided information and images for this book:

Anne Chiarelli Jones and Denise Morrison of the Kansas City Museum/Union Station; Sharman Robertson of the Hallmark Archives; Janet Russell of the Jackson County Historical Society Archives in Independence; Roger Berg Jr. of the Toy & Miniature Museum; Robert Ray of the Miller Nichols Library Special Collections at the University of Missouri-Kansas City; David Boutros and his staff at the Western Historical Manuscript Collection-Kansas City, and the staff of the Special Collections Department at the Kansas City Public Library.

BIBLIOGRAPHY

Books

Barnett, James H. *American Christmas: A Study in National Culture*. New York: The MacMillan Co., 1954.

Brewerton, G. Douglas. *Wars of the Western Border; or, New Homes and a Strange People*. New York: Derby & Jackson, 1857.

Bruce, Janet. *The John Wornall House. 1858: The History and Restoration of Kansas City's Historic Wornall House Museum*. Independence: Jackson County Historical Society, 1983.

Kane, Harnett T. *The Southern Christmas Book: The Full Story from Earliest Times to Present: People, Customs, Conviviality, Carols, Cooking*. New York: David McKay Company Inc., 1958.

Garraghan, Gilbert J., S.J. *Catholic Beginnings in Kansas City, Missouri: An Historical Sketch*. Chicago: Loyola University Press, 1920.

Green, Lorenzo J. et al. *Missouri's Black Heritage*. Revised edition. Columbia: University of Missouri Press, 1993.

Gulevich, Tanya. *Encyclopedia of Christmas*. Detroit: Omnigraphics, 2000.

Hadfield, Miles and John. *The Twelve Days of Christmas*. Boston: Little, Brown and Company, 1961.

Nissenbaum, Stephen. *The Battle for Christmas*. New York: Alfred A. Knopf, 1996.

McDermott, John Francis. *Travels in Search of the Elephant: The Wanderings of Alfred S. Wauch, Artist, in Louisiana, Missouri, and Santa Fe, in 1845-1846*. St. Louis: Missouri Historical Society, 1951.

Marling, Karal Ann. *Merry Christmas! Celebrating America's Greatest Holiday*. Cambridge, Mass.: Harvard University Press, 2000.

Marra, Dorothy Brandt. *This Far by Faith. Vol. 1. The Story*. Kansas City: Diocese of Kansas City-St. Joseph, 1992.

Miles, Clement A. *Christmas in Ritual and Tradition, Christian and Pagan*. London: Adelphi Terrace, T. Fisher Unwin, 1912 (Republished by Gale Research Co., Book Tower, Detroit, 1968.)

Montgomery, Rick and Kasper, Shirl. *Kansas City: An American Story*. Kansas City: Kansas City Star Books, 1999.

Paxton, W.M. *Annals of Platte County, Missouri*. Kansas City: Hudson Kimberly Publishing Co., 1897 (Reprinted by Platte County Historical Society Inc., Platte City, Mo., 1990).

History of Clay and Platte Counties, Missouri. St. Louis: National Historical Co., 1885 (Reprinted by Platte County Historical and Genealogical Society Inc., Platte City, Mo., 1989).

Restad, Penne L. *Christmas in America: A History*. New York: Oxford University Press, 1995.

Samuelson, Sue. *Christmas: An Annotated Bibliography*. New York: Garland Publishing, Inc., 1982.

Waits, William B. *The Modern Christmas in America: A Cultural History of Gift Giving*. New York and London: New York University Press, 1993.

Yetman, Norman R. *Life Under the "Peculiar Institution:" Selections from the Slave Narrative Collection*. New York: Holt, Rinehart and Winston Inc., 1970.

Newspaper files

The Kansas City Star.
The Kansas City Times.
The Kansas City Mail.
The Border Star of Westport, Mo.
The *Journal of Commerce* of Kansas City. This name of this newspaper was rendered variously through the years as the *Western Journal of Commerce*, the *Kansas City Daily Western Journal of Commerce* and several other ways. *The Enterprise* was its name when it was founded. In the 20th century, it was called the *Kansas City Journal* and the *Kansas City Journal-Post*.
The Tribune of Liberty, Mo.
The Mirror of Olathe, Kan.

Articles

Caldwell, Dorothy J. "Christmas in Early Missouri." *Missouri Historical Review*. Vol. 65, January 1971.

Hoole, William Stanley, ed. "A Southerner's Viewpoint of the Kansas Situation, 1856-1857." *The Kansas Historical Quarterly*. Vol. 3, February 1934.

Owen, Mary Alicia. "Social Customs and Usages in Missouri During the Last Century." *Missouri Historical Review*. Vol. 15, October 1920.

Rice, Cyrus R. "Experiences of a Pioneer Missionary." *Collections of the Kansas State Historical Society, 1913,1914*. Vol. 13. 1915.

Squires, Monas K. "Merry-Making in Missouri in the Old Days." *The Missouri Historical Review*. Vol. 28, January 1934.

White, Mrs. S.B. "My First Days in Kansas." *Collections of the Kansas State Historical Society, 1909-1910*. Vol. 11, 1910.

ILLUSTRATION SOURCES

Images from the files of *The Kansas City Star* for which a photographer or artist can be identified are listed below, as well as images from other archives. Images from *Star* files for which credit cannot be determined are not listed below.

Dust jacket front: Warner Studio Collection, courtesy Kansas City Museum/Union Station. Back: Beverly Bynum, *The Star*.

Endsheets: Kansas City Museum/Union Station and Toy & Minature Museum of Kansas City.

ii-iii. Jackson County Historical Society Archives.

vi-vii. Missouri Division of Tourism.

viii. Wendy Yang, *The Star*.

x. Black Archives of Mid-America.

xi. Keith Myers, *The Star*.

xii. Beverly Bynum, *The Star*.

xiv-1. Courtesy of the Hallmark Archives, Hallmark Cards, Inc.

4. Special Collections, Kansas City Public Library, Kansas City, Missouri.

8. "Depart de Westport:" Historical Photograph Collections, Washington State University Libraries.

9. Courtesy American Antiquarian Society.

10. Toy & Miniature Museum of Kansas City.

14. Left: Western Historical Manuscript Collection-Kansas City.

14-15. Used by permission, State Historical Society of Missouri, Columbia.

20. Kansas State Historical Society.

21. Special Collections, Kansas City Public Library, Kansas City, Missouri.

23. Kansas City Museum/Union Station.

24. Toy & Miniature Museum of Kansas City.

26-27. Map collections, Library of Congress.

28-29. Used by permission of the University of Missouri-Kansas City Libraries, Special Collections Department.

35. Toy & Miniature Museum of Kansas City.

38,39. Courtesy of the Hallmark Archives, Hallmark Cards, Inc.

40. Used by permission of the University of Missouri-Kansas City Libraries, Special Collections Department.

42. Left: Special Collections, Kansas City Public Library, Kansas City, Missouri.

42-43. Western Historical Manuscript Collection-Kansas City.

44. Lower left: Jackson County Historical Society Archives.

46. Special Collections, Kansas City Public Library, Kansas City, Missouri.

47. Courtesy of the Hallmark Archives, Hallmark Cards, Inc.

48. Jackson County Historical Society Archives.

49. Western Historical Manuscript Collection-Kansas City.

53. Right: Kansas City Museum/Union Station, Kansas City, Missouri.

54. Center: Toy & Miniature Museum of Kansas City. Top right: Jackson County Historical Society Archives.

55. Top left: Special Collections, Kansas City Public Library, Kansas City, Missouri.; Remainder: Jackson County Historical Society Archives.

56. Top: Toy & Miniature Museum of Kansas City. Bottom: Jackson County Historical Society Archives.

57. Fred Harvey Collection photographs, Box 6, Special Collections, The University of Arizona Library.

59. Kansas City Museum/Union Station, Kansas City, Missouri.

64. Jackson County Historical Society Archives.

65. Western Historical Manuscript Collection-Kansas City.

66. Kansas City Museum/Union Station.

67. Wilborn & Associates.

68. Wilborn & Associates.

69. Top: Special Collections, Kansas City Public Library, Kansas City, Missouri. Bottom: Wilborn & Associates.

70. Top: Wilborn & Associates. Bottom: Western Historical Manuscript Collection-Kansas City.

71. Top: Wilborn & Associates. Bottom left: Western Historical Manuscript Collection-Kansas City. Bottom right: Special Collections, Kansas City Public Library, Kansas City, Missouri.

74. Cards courtesy of the Hallmark Archives, Hallmark Cards, Inc.

75. Gift wrap: Toy & Miniature Museum, Kansas City. Catalogue: Jackson County Historical Society Archives.

76,77. Toy & Miniature Museum, Kansas City.

78. Store interior and cards: Courtesy of the Hallmark Archives, Hallmark Cards, Inc.

79. Top: Western Historical Manuscript Collection-Kansas City. Bottom right: Jackson County Historical Society Archives.

81. Top: Courtesy City Union Mission.

82. Top: Western Historical Manuscript Collection-Kansas City. Bottom: Kansas City Museum/Union Station.

83. Kansas City Museum/Union Station.

84. Top: Special Collections, Kansas City Public Library, Kansas City, Missouri. Bottom: Toy & Miniature Museum, Kansas City.

86. Top and middle: Kansas City Museum/Union Station.

87. Top: Crown Center.

89. Used by permission of the University of Missouri-Kansas City Libraries, Special Collections Department.

90. Courtesy of the Hallmark Archives, Hallmark Cards, Inc.

91. Collection of Marjorie Siegrist Ebling.

92. Bottom: Used by permission of the University of Missouri-Kansas City Libraries, Special Collections Department.

93. Wilborn & Associates.

94. Toy & Miniature Museum, Kansas City.

98. Kansas City Museum/Union Station.

100. Bottom: Kansas City Museum/Union Station.

101. Bottom: Kansas City Museum/Union Station.

103. Bottom right: Toy & Miniature Museum, Kansas City.

104. Jackson County Historical Society Archives.

105. Black Archives of Mid-America.

106. Top: Jackson County Historical Society Archives. Bottom left: Wilborn & Associates.

107. Warner Studio Collection, courtesy Kansas City Museum/Union Station.

108. Kansas City Museum/Union Station.

111. Toy & Miniature Museum, Kansas City.

114,115. Courtesy of the Hallmark Archives, Hallmark Cards, Inc.

116. William E. Humphrey, *The Star*.

117. Craig Sands, *The Star*.

118. Paul Iwanaga, *The Kansas City Times*.

122. Top: Wilborn & Associates. Bottom: Roger Reynolds, *The Star*.

123. William H. Batson, *The Kansas City Times*.

124. Joe Ledford, *The Star*.

125. Top, Talis Bergmanis, *The Star*. Bottom: Carole Archer, *The Kansas City Times*.

126. Peggy Bair, *The Star*.

127. Top: Ray Corey, *The Star*. Bottom: Fred Blocher, *The Star*.

128. Dick Mackey, *Star and Times*.

129. Tammy Ljungblad, *The Star*.

130. Toy & Miniature Museum, Kansas City.

131. Jim McTaggart, *The Star*.

133. Rich Sugg, *The Star*.

134-135. Lighted house: Beverly Bynum, *The Star*.

135. Peggy Bair, *The Star*.

136. Stephen B. Thornton, *The Star*.

137. Top: Beverly Bynum; bottom: Jeffery Washington. Both of *The Star*.

138. Clockwise from left: Anne Marie Hunter, Julie Jacobson and Todd Feeback, all of *The Star*.

139. Clockwise from top: David Brandt, Rich Sugg and Andy Nelson, all of *The Star*.

140-141. Steve Gonzales, *The Star*.

142. Top: Fred Blocher, *The Star*. Bottom: Brian Crites, *The Star*.

143. Lee Judge, *The Star*.

144-145. Jim McTaggart, *The Star*.

146. Craig Sands, *The Star*.

147. Marcio Jose Sanchez, *The Star*.

148. Anne Marie Hunter.

149. Beverly Bynum, *The Star*.

150. Craig Sands, *The Star*.

151. Jim Larson.

152. Mari Ogawa, *The Star*.

153. Susan Pfanmuller.

154. Craig Sands, *The Star*.

155. Talis Bergmanis, *The Star*.

156-157. Peggy Bair, *The Star*.

158. Beverly Bynum, *The Star*.

INDEX

A

Alameda Plaza Hotel, 116

B

Babick, Mike, 135
Battle of Westport, 26
Beronius, Dale, 88, 102
Board of Public Welfare, 51
Brett, George, 116, 118, 119

C

Chiefs, Kansas City, 128
Chouteau, Francois, 4, 6
Christianity, early, 5
Christmas
    advertising, 20, 21, 29, 31, 40, 45, 54, 100, 129
    balls, 11, 14, 19, 24
    baubles and bulbs, 98
    burn-out, 58
    carols, 105
    catalogs, 75
    charitable events, 42, 44, 51
    children and, 13, 37, 150
    Christmas clubs, 53
    clothing, 100
    community tree, 60
    dancing, 11, 26, 28
    dinners, 34, 46, 48, 50, 153
    displays, 68, 69, 135
    drinking, 12, 19, 23, 35, 36
    electric lights, 31, 48
    fireworks, 25, 32
    food, 13, 22, 28
    gift-wrapping, 47
    gifts, 17, 33, 40
    greeting cards, 38, 42, 44, 54, 55, 74, 78, 90, 114, 115
    letters to Santa Claus, 56
    lighting, 101, 103, 105, 121
    magic of, 3
    marketing campaigns, 64
    memories, 59, 97
    merchants, 14, 37, 54, 57, 68, 86, 98, 104, 105, 129
    movies, 130
    opposition to, 7
    parades, 70, 72, 113
    retailers, 20, 31, 64, 54, 69
    Santa's Wonderland, 122
    slaves' celebration of, 16
    songs, 89
    tamales, 147
    toys, 10, 24, 32, 100, 103, 111, 130
    tree, 30, 48, 66, 131
    tuba Christmas concert, 152
Christmas Carol, A, 44, 127
churches, 34, 87, 103
    African Methodist Episcopal, 34
    Cathedral of the Immaculate Conception, 87
    First Christian Church, 133
    Grace and Holy Trinity Cathedral, 88
    Grace Assembly of God, 148
    Queen of the Holy Rosary, 146
    Reorganized Church of Jesus Christ of Latter-Day Saints, 94
    Second Presbyterian, 34
    St. Patrick's, 34
    Village Presbyterian, 103
City Union Mission, 81, 84
Civil War, 25
Claus, Santa, 9, 24, 56, 66, 73, 111, 138, 139, 140, 142
Coates Opera House, 34
Connor, Patrick, 62, 63
Country Club Plaza, 64, 70, 71, 100, 101, 102, 111, 116, 119, 120, 145
    lights, 70, 101, 117, 118, 120
Crown Drug Co., 79
Cuddles and Tuckie, 96

D

Davis, Ilus W., 116
Dickens, Charles, 44
Donnelly Garment Co., 84

E

Emery, Bird, Thayer Co., 57, 75, 76, 87, 100, 110
    mechanical Santa, 87

G

Gillham Park, 122, 142
Good Fellows, 53

H

Hall brothers, 54
Hall, Joyce, 47
Hall's, 78, 105
Hallmark, 114, 130; *Hall of Fame*, 130
Helping Hand Institute, 84
Holcombe, Gary, 129

J

Jessee, Randall, 103
John Taylor Dry Goods Co., 80
Jones Store Co., 57, 68, 78, 80, 109
Judge, Lee, 143

K

Kansas City,
    population, 28, 37, 66, 86
    suburbs, 105
Kansas City bridge, 28
Kansas Territory, 17, 19, 24
Kawsmouth, 4, 6, 8
Kline's department store, 79, 86, 108, 109
    Fairy Princess, 86, 108

M

Mayor's Christmas activities, 42, 46, 47, 51, 52, 54, 67, 82, 83, 87, 90, 122, 123, 154,
Mayerberg, Rabbi Samuel S., 89
Missouri Repertory Theatre, 127, 129
model steam railroad locomotives, 84
Municipal Auditorium, 90

N

native Americans, 10
Nicholas, St., 9, 24
Nichols, J.C., 70
Nichols, Miller, 120

P

Pendergast, Thomas J., 81, 84
Point, Father Nicholas, 8
poor, the, 41, 49, 51
Prohibition, 85
Puritans, 7

R

Roux, Father Benedict, 6, 8
Rudolph, the Red-Nosed Reindeer, 102

S

Salvation Army, 42, 48, 49, 127
Sears Roebuck and Co., 100
Shawnee Indian Mission, 20
shopping, 66, 100, 104, 137
    centers and malls: Antioch, 108; Bannister, 137; Blue Ridge, 108, 109; French Market, 109; Independence, 109; Indian Springs, 109; Metcalf South, 109; Metro North, 109; Oak Park, 109; Prairie Village, 108; Truman Corners, 108; Ward Parkway, 108, 155
    Downtown Kansas City, 65, 103, 104, 106, 109, 110, 111
    Petticoat Lane, 69, 98, 99, 106
    Troost Avenue, 69, 70, 104
snow, 18, 61, 62, 63
Snowflake, 64
Social Gospel, 41, 44, 48
streetcars, 79

T

teddy bears, 56
Three-Star Club, 93
Toy Town, 76, 100
Truman, Harry S., 94, 95, 111

U

Union Depot, 40
Union Station, 57, 60, 67, 68, 101
USO, 92

V

V-Mail, 92
Vaughan, Bill, 156

W

Walnut Street, 69
WDAF, 64, 66, 96, 103
weather, 18
Wheeler, Charles, 116
World War I, 57, 60, 64
World War II, 87, 88, 90, 98

Y

yule log, 16